I LEARNT ABOUT FLYING F

A Collection of Articles from 'Air Clues', the RAF Magazine

'Wing Commander Spry' and Lindsay Peacock

Published by The RAF Benevolent Fund Enterprises

I Learnt About Flying From That

Published by: The Royal Air Force
Benevolent Fund Enterprises,
Building 15, RAF Fairford,
Glos GL7 4DL, England

Publishing Director: Paul A Bowen
Publishing Coordinator: Karen Pell

Compiled & Edited: Wing Commander Spry, Lindsay Peacock, Karen Pell
Photographs Courtesy of: PRM Aviation
Illustrations: Les Cooper (LC), Flight Lieutenant Gary Weightman (GW),
Chief Technician Chris Gransden (CG)

Typesetting & Design: Sharron Lawrence
Cover design: Les Cooper

ISBN 1-899808-75-2

Printed in Hong Kong

FOREWORD

There are few certainties in life, but of one thing I am sure - we all need to learn from our mistakes. However, life is too short to make all the mistakes yourself; therefore, it is vital to learn from those of others. But we can only do this if we talk about our mistakes in the first place.

In the hustle and bustle of modern life there seems, regrettably, to be less time to swap stories and listen to the experiences of those around us. That is why this book is so important. The many authors who have contributed to this 'I Learnt About Flying From That' book have provided a wealth of stories and give an insight into some telling experiences. Some of the stories are extremely funny while others are tragic; but they all contain that vital element - the feeling for the reader that 'it could have been me'.

Enjoy the articles and place yourself in the shoes of the authors. They learnt from their mistakes and lived to tell the tale.

RICHARD BRANSON
AUGUST 1996

INTRODUCTION

As the Inspector of Flight Safety for the Royal Air Force, I am delighted to see this book published, not just because I think it will be of interest to a wide audience, whether involved with aviation or not, but also because I think you will find it entertaining, thought provoking and fascinating reading. We have been publishing 'I learnt about flying from that' stories in the RAF magazine 'Air Clues' since the 1940's, when articles were written for what was then intended to be a short term series. Indeed the first article in this book was the first ever submitted. Over 50 years later I am still receiving these short stories from aircrew who want to share their experiences. In all, I have a library of over 300 stories from which we have selected 60 for this particular book. I hope that the book will be the forerunner of further editions because there is more to tell and more to learn. The stories in this book cover many generations of flying and I am indebted to all those who have written about their experiences. Many of their stories are, or will become, aviation folklore. I hope also that in producing this book it might prompt others to write about their experiences. It is only when we hear about these that we can learn and thus help prevent accidents in the future. Indirectly, therefore, I see the production of this book as being beneficial to the prevention of flying accidents.

Many people have been involved in the production of this book in addition to the original authors of the stories themselves. My thanks go to those involved in the early discussions, in particular to Air Commodore Andy Griffin and my then deputy, Group Captain 'Dim' Jones. I am sure that Andy would have taken on the project himself if I and my staff had not reacted favourably to the idea. I am grateful to my staff for the work done in their own time to prepare the material for the book, especially Squadron Leader John Chapman, my head of publicity and the current Wing Commander Spry, and his then assistant, Flying Officer Alun Pepper. Flight Lieutenant Gary Weightman, Chief Technician Chris Gransden and my graphics artist, Mr Les Cooper, have together helped illustrate the book. They have done a magnificent job and demonstrated their individual and considerable talents. The Royal Air Force Benevolent Enterprises have been most helpful throughout and have overseen the publishing of the book. The proceeds of the book will go to the RAF Benevolent Fund, a most worthy cause. Particular thanks must go to Mr Paul Bowen and Mrs Karen Pell of RAF Benevolent Fund Enterprises.

Finally, I am delighted that Richard Branson kindly agreed to write the Foreword. He is not only famous for the creation of his VIRGIN empire, and in particular the airline that carries the name, but he is himself an aviation adventurer. His exploits associated with breaking aviation records in hot air balloons have been widely publicised. I am sure that like all aviators, he has his own 'I learnt about flying from that' experiences and I find it most appropriate that he has associated himself with this book.

AIR CDRE R S PEACOCK-EDWARDS CBE AFC FIMgt RAF
INSPECTOR OF FLIGHT SAFETY (ROYAL AIR FORCE)

CONTENTS

GW

HEADING INTO TROUBLE

Hawker Typhoon 1B

At the end of the war in Europe, the silly season got under way in earnest. It was a time when anything went: low flying, beat-ups from air to ground... and even a mock fight between the Officers' and Sergeants' Messes at Ahlhorn in which live ammunition was used - until a bullet went through a window and ricocheted round the room of a non-participant who was writing a quiet letter home. You name it, we did it.

Our airfield was regularly beaten-up by a couple of American P-47 Thunderbolts that screamed across at nought feet. Not surprisingly, we swore to 'do' them when we found out where they came from.

One warm afternoon I had just got airborne in a Typhoon and was climbing out of the circuit when I saw some of our American cousins 'at it' below me. What a chance to even things up! I followed them at a safe distance and saw them land and taxy in at Cassel, at which point I began to show off something rotten.

I dived on everything in sight. I flew between hangars, missed buildings by what I thought was inches, and when I tired of the sport I pulled up in a steep climb at full power to go home. Imagine my horror when I noticed a couple of 'them' orbiting well up and obviously waiting to give me 'the works'. Already climbing steeply, I gaped at them over my shoulder, unwittingly pulling on the stick and applying rudder as I stared up and back. The inevitable sucker's spin followed and the Typhoon went down rather faster than it had gone up. Normal recovery action worked but the pull-out skimmed the tops of the trees at the bottom of a narrow valley; there wasn't an inch to spare in any direction and it was pure luck that I got away with it. I took care to climb away carefully this time, but couldn't help wondering why my feet were beating a tattoo on the cockpit floor and why I was sweating profusely. It must have been sheer fright. I only hoped that the Americans would regard it as the most skilful piece of evasive action they had ever seen. They would never know . . .

I estimated a heading for base of 015° and set off. The countryside began to look unfamiliar and some haze developed. Calls for bearings got no reply. I was lost and, not wanting to push my luck too far, I landed at the first likely looking strip. Close to some apparently occupied huts I switched off and was very soon surrounded by a horde of ill-kept, sad-looking men and women. One of them spoke sufficient English to make me understand that I was at Gotha in the Russian Sector and I also learned that the airfield was occupied by displaced persons.

A heading of 015° would have taken me home, but for some reason I had steered 115° and here I was - in a predicament. Within minutes, a soldier with a red star on his cap appeared on an old hand-gear motorbike and pointed to the pillion seat. I got on. After a short ride, we stopped outside an office in the town. Three soldiers sat on the kerb and rolled what might have been dice in the gutter. Inside the building, I noticed three rifles propped behind the door. Well, their war was over and relaxation had been earned. We were still engaged with Japan so they may have been legally permitted to hang on to me.

With a mixture of signs, drawings, and inadequate German, I tried to indicate that I was lost because my compass was unserviceable, but now that I knew where I was I would be able to follow the autobahn to the American Sector. I got the impression that their Town Major or equivalent (who was interviewing me) thought I intended taxying along the road and he would escort me. He scrutinised my maps, which now lay open on his desk, said something to my escort and I was then taken along the outside passage and put in a room. The door closed and the key turned quietly. I was not completely isolated, however; a hatch in the wall opened and a plate came through with a piece of brown bread and some pickled cucumber which I promptly ate to show my appreciation. Dessert was a packet of ersatz cigarettes which I smoked somewhat apprehensively. My apprehension was genuine, especially after five rather smarter looking soldiers came in, had a look at me and then went out again. The thought crossed my mind that they might do something unfriendly.

After an hour or so, the boss came in with my maps. He pointed to the door and ushered me to a waiting staff car. Not a word was spoken as we drove back to the airfield and stopped a few yards from the Typhoon. The poor old Typhy was by now covered with camp inmates. They were everywhere - in the cockpit, on the wings - two were even sitting on the mainwheels contentedly puffing away at cigarettes. Our motor cyclist had followed us and he shooed them away. The officer with my maps sat on the car bumper and had a think; then, he suddenly put the maps in my hand and said the only word of English I heard him utter - "Go!". I was in the cockpit in a flash and damned lucky that, with no ground crew, the engine went first time. There was no windsock so I lined up along the longest clear patch of grass and pushed the throttle to the stop.

This time, I checked my heading properly and got within radio range of Hildesheim some hours after I should have run out of fuel. My story that I had got lost in thick haze was accepted (I think) and I heard no more of that day until about 12 years later when I was relaying the story to some fellow instructors. One of them said, "I knew I'd seen you somewhere before. I authorised your trip that day!"

GW

BY GEORGE THAT WAS CLOSE

Many years ago during the War, I qualified at CFS and instructing became an aspect of my career that I really enjoyed. After my first tour in Bomber Command, I started teaching young pilots on Whitleys. I felt it was right and proper that I should pass on whatever experience I had and it is to this end that I am now recounting an experience of which I am thoroughly ashamed. My Pathfinder crew had no idea of what happened at the time and they never found out, for they were all killed on the first sortie they flew after I was 'hijacked' from my Squadron to be a staff officer at Pathfinder Group Headquarters.

Short Stirling

Let me set the scene. It was 1943 and the Pathfinders had been going for some months. Gradually, we were getting closer to our targets and electronic devices were coming along which would improve our navigation, which was the be-all and end-all of Pathfinding. My tale relates to one night early that year. It was my task to lead the Squadron off to somewhere in the Ruhr and we were on the short runway at Oakington. We had instilled in all of us a very strong sense of timing, which had to be to the second, and this had become a habit. So, as a rule, I would always get off the chocks in plenty of time and would get very testy if things weren't exactly right come take-off time.

On this occasion, something delayed me and I was late. I was in command of a heavily-laden Stirling - an aircraft that was renowned for the fact that on a cold night the engines took a long time to warm up, even with the gills closed. The orders were very strict that one could not move off until the oil temperature was above the minimum, but I was quite determined to make up lost time. I got out to the end of the runway first, applied my brakes and did the usual run-up and magneto checks, whilst waiting impatiently for the oil temperature to rise to the required degree. The Flight Engineer complained bitterly as I was making the preparations for take-off, but I ignored him. The Navigator was giving me the count-down; as soon as the needles on the oil temperature gauge started moving I would be off, making sure I got airborne on time as this would be vital for the rest of the Squadron. I was very proud of the reputation I had earned for punctuality.

Take-off time arrived and the oil temperatures were still somewhat below the criteria, but I opened the throttles anyway. Very shortly, the tail was up and I was heading down the short runway into a brisk headwind, pointing straight at the little pub outside the camp that had become a second home for all of us. The wheels lifted off the runway, up came the undercarriage and, as it was the short runway, I left the flaps down a little longer than usual. To my absolute horror, I found that all my controls were completely frozen, despite the fact that I was quite certain I had seen the ground crew go round and remove all the external locks before I boarded the Stirling.

We were climbing away at a very gentle angle and I could not understand why I was unable to move the controls. Fortunately, the aircraft maintained a perfect climbing attitude while I tried to sort it out. I reached for the elevator trim wheel; one glance told me it was in the normal position. We were still climbing at full power and a touch of nose-up trim enabled me to increase the rate of climb. As my hand came away from the trim wheel I touched the autopilot control and, on looking down, I was shocked to see that it was engaged; I had taken off with 'George' in control.

Being one of the most experienced pilots in Bomber Command and having done an instructional tour meant nothing. In my hurry, and in the conceit that is deep within many pilots with our belief in our own infallibility, I hadn't done my pre-take off checks thoroughly.

I was able to climb to about 1200 ft, at which height I felt it was safe enough for me to control any sudden change of attitude when I disengaged the autopilot. Fortunately, when I did, we maintained a perfect climbing attitude. I duly completed the mission, but I spent some time thinking about the young airman who had done the daily inspection of the instruments and who had left the autopilot engaged. However, I should still have done the proper cockpit checks, which I certainly did ever after. Fortune smiled on me and my crew that night, and what could have been a disaster was averted.

Despite my wealth of experience and time as an instructor, I had become over-confident in my own ability. My crew were never aware of the lapse and I am just as ashamed to recount this story today as I would have been had I told it 45 years ago. The lessons are of course, don't be distracted and DON'T ASSUME - CHECK.

CRAMPED FOR STYLE

Early in the war I was at Elementary Flying Training School and was rapidly becoming a confident pilot with a massive 41 hrs on Tiger Moths. My ego was further inflated by my instructor telling me that the task for the following day was spins and stalls - but, 'solo'! He also, after much verbal warning, told me I could do a loop if I wished.

Let us now return to the evening before the great event. I was taking part in a scratch game of rugby football when I received a kick on the left calf muscle. That night I gave the resulting bruise a hot soak and massage, and the next morning, although my leg felt a little sore, it was not inconveniencing me in any way.

I climbed into the rear cockpit of the Tiger, started up, performed the usual checks and commenced my take-off run. The tail came up, I was approaching flying speed, and all was going swimmingly when I got a sudden terrific cramp in my left calf muscle. I instinctively straightened my leg to ease the pain, overlooking the fact that my foot happened to be on the rudder bar at the time.

As my instructor later remarked, a left hand climbing take-off was not in the curriculum, although I recall that he put it rather more forcefully than that. Yes, I managed to get off the ground and return, but the dampness on my forehead certainly wasn't caused by the outside air temperature.

CG

A JOUST TOO FAR

The date was October 1944. I was a junior member of No 140 Squadron flying PR Mosquitos. We were part of 34 Wing 2nd Tactical Air Force operating out of Melsbroek (Brussels) and were suffering casualties as a result of the Me262s in particular. Until they and the He163s came on the scene, in roughly mid-1944, the going had been reasonable.

Since we were unarmed, and therefore had to rely for our safety on out-manoeuvring the enemy, I formed the wholly unreasonable view that it would be a good thing if I had at least some idea of the capabilities of a single-seater fighter. The more so since I had never flown a single other than a Tiger Moth - quite a few twins and even fours, but never a fighter.

Spitfire Mk XI

I had, curiously enough in retrospect, a strange instinct for survival, so I mounted a sustained attack on the CO of No 16 Squadron with the object of being allowed to fly one of his Spitfires, hopefully in mock combat with one of his more experienced pilots, to determine:

- ✈ What they could do
- ✈ What one should do in a Mosquito to frustrate the enemy.

My campaign was successful, though why the CO ever allowed one of his precious aircraft to be given into my heavy-handed charge I never did find out. At all events, he allocated a senior flight commander to instruct me in the cockpit drill and told him to make himself available for one hour's mock aerial combat.

Any pilot can imagine my excitement at being allowed this privilege. The Flight Commander was a Canadian (subsequently president of a large Canadian public company, and still a firm friend) who, understandably, took a slightly jaundiced view of this unwanted chore.

We had, as I recall, a somewhat cold and formal meeting, during which he handed me the Pilot's Notes to study and learn by heart. Once I had absorbed that information, he gave me a practical test in the cockpit of a Spitfire XI. Satisfied, albeit reluctantly, with my mastery of all this, he announced that he would board the adjacent aircraft; we would then start up, taxy out, take off, fly a climbing course of 280° and start our simulated combat over Bruges. I was to lead; he was to follow and give advice. By then, I was having doubts as to the wisdom of the whole operation, especially as I couldn't see anything ahead at all, despite being tallish and perching on a parachute and a rubber dinghy. He said: "Never mind, taxy out and zig zag - you'll see plenty when the tail comes up. By the way, when you take off and land, keep the right-hand edge of the runway under the middle of the starboard aileron - it gives you a sense of direction".

With that, he hopped into his aircraft. We started up, established radio contact, and got permission to taxy out and take off on Runway 20. (Remember the runway number, it is important). The whole thing was fantastic. I reached the runway, lined up (starboard wing over-hanging the runway edge) and very slowly increased the power. I had the stick right forward to get the tail up quickly. Talk about response and over-correction! Everything I did, I did too much of. The tail came up beyond the horizontal, I over-corrected the swing; the speed mounted to 90 kts in a flash.

I hauled her off somehow, pulled up the undercarriage, closed the canopy, held the ASI at 90, pulled the revs back to 2,700 from 3,000 and, at last beginning to sort myself out, found myself climbing at an apparent angle of 45° at 1500 ft. The good Canadian wisely kept a safe distance behind and to port, observing only that I had apparently tried to emulate a grasshopper, so erratic were my movements.

We were locked in the ecstacy of esoteric aerial combat over Bruges at around 15,000 ft when an oil seal ruptured in my propeller constant speed unit; consequently my windscreen and canopy suddenly went black. I told the good Canadian that I had a visibility problem, to which he replied that I must slow down, pull the canopy back, half open the cockpit door to lock it open, and not, repeat not, formate on him, but instead maintain station at a minimum of 100 yds behind and to his port. He would then lead me back to base, seek permission to land, and cross over the signal area at 1500 ft, at right angles to the runway. Thereafter, when he announced that I was on my own, I could look down to my left, confirm the direction of landing and go into a slowly descending left-hand half-gliding turn, which would give me a good view (sideways) of the proceedings.

I agreed to all this, but the curious thing was that I distinctly heard the air traffic controller give permission to land on Runway 02. Furthermore, the T in the square confirmed 02 as the active runway. Consequently, I went into a long descending turn and ended up at nought feet, with my starboard aileron hanging over the edge of the starboard side of the runway. At that juncture, I closed the throttle and pulled the stick back more and more. I was just comfortably settling into a beautiful three-point landing, when there was a sudden sort of 'bumph' and I saw out of the corner of my left eye (and felt) a Spitfire flash past me on the runway, going quite rapidly in the opposite direction. Some pretty horrible comments were broadcast on the radio but nothing could destroy my deep satisfaction at having accomplished such a perfect three-pointer.

CG

If there is a moral to this tale, it is that you should assume nothing (like, if you take off in one direction, it does not mean that you must land in the same direction) and that, while you should listen, understand and do what you are told, you should also seek clarification if you have any doubts.

Perhaps it also pays to do precisely as you are told. I did, in particular, hang my starboard wing over the right-hand edge of the runway, while my Canadian friend did (and this is rare) exactly what he had told me to do. Thus, we passed harmlessly - but it could all have ended so differently.

STRAPPED FOR DASH

Having completed my training and a double tour on Meteors and Hunters, I re-entered the pilot training world at the end of the 1950s as a B2 QFI. I was amazed by all the new rules and regulations that had sprung up in Flying Training Command and the generation of 'old' QFIs who had inherited the flight and squadron commanders' jobs. They preached rigid adherence to the rules and (in my jaundiced view) were breeding a generation of straight and level bomber pilots rather than the press-on fighter aces that I thought the Royal Air Force really needed. I therefore felt it my duty to inculcate into my students the necessary dash and determination to view all FOBs, ASIs, AMFOs (later MODFOs, then MFRs) and other assorted rules with disdain, if not quite complete disregard.

Towards the end of my three year stint as a QFI, having converted from Piston Provosts to Jet Provosts, I inherited a rather shy, nervous and unlikely student pilot, named Jerry, who was under review and in danger of being 'chopped'. My professional ability was at stake, not to mention personal pride. Therefore, as an A2, I would get him through - first of all by superior instruction (not that rubbish propounded in AP3225) and, secondly, by turning him into a 'press-on' fighter type, full of dash and determination to do or die. All he needed was a good example to model himself on!

Our Relief Landing Ground (RLG) was some 15 miles from base and was a pleasant place to depart to when the dual-to-solo circuit-bashing phase of the course was on. That particular July day I was over there with my protege and, after he had made the requisite three safe approaches and landings, I got out and sat in the Tower, drinking tea with the controller. My student and three others then lurched round the circuit - frightening themselves and each other - until it was time to come in and refuel. My lad was due in last and, despite a call over the radio, was still merrily going round and round long after the other three had landed. Still, 5 o'clock was drawing near so I had him called in and requested a fuel check. The 'Rules' said there must be 800 lb remaining before leaving the RLG; he had 650 lb. Anyway, the aged civilian bowser and its equally aged operator were almost empty and tired (respectively), so why waste time refuelling when all you needed was a maximum of 200 lb to go straight home? That was my first mistake.

I climbed on to the starboard wing and, with the engine running and the hood open, started to take off the canvas cover over my ejection seat. Jerry tapped his hand on the fuel gauge. I leaned over and took a good look. The gauge read just over 450 lb. "Not to worry"; I shouted, "that's plenty to get home with", reasoning that this would show him some of the true fighter pilot's 'press-on' spirit. To save wasting more fuel, I then did something that even to this day makes me cringe. I got into the cockpit and sat on top of the canvas-covered ejection seat, plugged in my lead and said "OK, I'll ride on the seat like this without strapping-in, so make sure you find the way home and don't get lost". We called "Taxying", did the pre-take-off checks on the roll and were 'airborne, to base local frequency' in no time flat.

Sitting in the sun after a busy but enjoyable day's work, I was pleasantly relaxed and enjoying the passing country-side from 1500 ft when my reverie was shattered by the radio message: "All aircraft stand-off. We have an obstruction on the runway. No further landings". The old fighter pilot mental reflexes leapt into life - runway obstructed - no further landings - us with not too much fuel - and me not strapped into my bang seat. I can report, authoritatively, that when airborne it is impossible to take the cover off the Martin-Baker Mk 4 ejection seat, get strapped in and remove the safety pins - believe you me, I tried hard to succeed as we orbited the airfield that afternoon.

Luckily, the obstruction was dragged clear in record time and by saying (nonchalantly, of course), "Rather short of fuel at this time, request priority", we made a safe and expeditious landing, taxied in and shut down. I said nothing to Jerry, and he said nothing to me. (I don't think I ever did debrief him on that sortie, and I can't recall ever writing up his F5060).

The following morning our Line Chief asked me if I'd had any trouble as the refuellers had signed-up for putting 2200 lb of fuel into my aircraft after our return the previous night. I replied casually, "No, no problem, your refueller must have made a mistake with the gauges. After all, the engine was still running when I taxied in - ho, ho, ho". He gave me an old-fashioned look and I passed on.

I had almost forgotten this incident until I met Jerry again some time later. He was a squadron leader and flight commander on a fighter unit. Despite not seeing each other for over 10 years, his first words as we shook hands were, "Hello Whiskers, tried strapping-in to any ejection seats lately?"

Obviously, he had 'learned about flying' from my crass stupidity and over-confidence that day. I certainly did, and for the remainder of my active flying in the RAF I checked that bang-seat and strapped it to my back like it was the best friend I ever had.

YEW CANNOT BE SERIOUS

The scene is 'Somewhere in Germany'. The period is 'Early Roaring Fifties'. The aircraft is the De Havilland Venom and the pilot is the archetypal steely 'hack 'em down' type, with the usual strong (but sometimes misguided) belief in his own immortality.

It was right in the middle of the silly season. Battle flight duty alternated with range programmes, high-level dog fights with low-level recces and wing Balbos with exercises. It was during one such exercise that our hero became unstuck - or rather, stuck - in that he hit the top of the only tree in the Army manoeuvre area during a low-level pass at the Pongos.

The collision was unfortunate for the pilot and his aircraft, but was even more catastrophic for the tree, since he hit it so hard that the top came off and embedded itself in the Venom's nose, from whence it could not be dislodged by any means. Our hero was therefore forced to return to base, peering anxiously through the surrounding foliage and with a nagging feeling that there were still more unpleasant surprises in the offing.

In the latter assumption, his fears proved unfounded, for the Station Commander happened to be away. As for the Wing Commander, once he had recovered from a severe fit of involuntary spasms induced by the sight of a tree with wings, he contented himself with a rocket which merely made our hero's eyes water even more.

And that, really, was that; although the real story is only now beginning. A few days after the tree-felling episode, the Squadron flew off to Sylt in Northern Germany. The main reason was for the annual Armament Practice Camp, although they were equally determined to sample the rival attractions offered by Sylt in summer. Naturally, these were indulged in wholeheartedly and, after an exuberant guest night, two of the staff and one Squadron member were detached to Hamburg's General Hospital for 'repairs'. It was at this point that our hero again came into the picture, by virtue of being one of the Squadron party to visit Hamburg for the Reeperbahn weekend.

They duly reached Hamburg late in the afternoon and, as the attractions in the notorious 'square mile' didn't really get into full swing until much later, they decided to visit their wounded comrade in hospital. There they found him, looking very sorry for himself and more than a little envious at missing the thrash that was to follow. The other two were equally mournful and, after doing the rounds and observing the social pleasantries, our hero came upon an even more forlorn figure - completely smothered in bandages and further inconvenienced by the fact that one leg was in traction.

"Wotcher", said our hero, to the incapacitated individual.

"Good afternoon", came the muffled reply.

"What's wrong with you?" our hero inquired, "Guest night?"

"Not really", said the figure. "Actually, I'm in the Army. I was injured by a tree during our last exercise".

"What tree?" asked our hero, with a start of alarm.

"The only tree for miles. I was standing under it when some idiot flew through it", the figure said, adding, "It fell on me".

There are indeed many strange ways in which one can learn about flying.

CG

THE FINAL TOUCHDOWN - ALMOST

De Havilland DH100 Vampire FB5

"Pride comes before a fall", goes the saying. How many times has pride been the cause of an aircraft accident, or a near accident? I know at least one instance of the latter because it was my pride which nearly caused me to depart the land of the living - prematurely and permanently.

It was a beautiful summer day in the mid-1950s and I was a student pilot at one of the Vampire Flying Training Schools. The course was well into one of the exciting phases - formation flying. The SOP was that we flew in a three-some with a QFI leading and two students as Nos 2 and 3, usually all in Mk 5s. One of the highlights of the exercise was the run-in and break, and we always tried to make it immaculate because we knew the rest of the course would be standing outside the crewroom watching for mistakes. Worse still, we knew they'd be ready with the usual raucous criticism if we botched it up.

On that fateful day, I was No 3 in the formation and, after a relatively successful session of aerobatics and tailchasing, we were running-in in echelon starboard to break for landing. We had briefed beforehand that the leader would land on the left side of the runway so that was where I should also land. All was going very well - nice tight echelon - and then the leader called "Breaking, breaking - Go", -2-3 then No 2 goes, -2-3- then it's my turn.

Pole hard over to the left, max rate roll to 90° bank, check, pull hard. At the same time close throttle, left hand straight down to the air brakes. Look out through the top of the canopy for the leader and No 2 - where the blazes is No 2 going? He's far too tight in to the runway, must be showing off his steep turn prowess; he'll never make it on to the runway from there - I'll stay outside him!

We carried on round the corner with the leader beautifully positioned, as always, No 2 apparently still inside him and yours truly, brimming over with self-confidence and scorn for my fellow student's lack of ability, outside No 2. But what's this? Here we are on finals with the leader crossing the hedge lined up on the left side of the runway and No 2, I don't believe it, perfectly lined up with the right hand side. Where am I? Lined up with the grass to the right of the runway!

Cue rapid departure of all that self-confidence and thoughts of one day becoming a fighter ace! I'd better go round again. But then I thought of the other students watching from outside the crewroom and the ribald comments I would get. No, I won't go round again, I can still get down OK. And so with less than 400 yards to the runway threshold I turned gently to cross behind No 2 and regain my rightful position on the left side. It was then that I hit his slipstream!

The subsequent events must have happened very quickly but time seemed to pass very slowly. The aircraft flicked over to almost 90° bank and started to slip in. My reactions may not have been entirely correct but they were certainly rapid - pole hard right, full top rudder, full throttle, and the aircraft responded. However, before it did, the port wing tip seemed to go through the top of the hedge, so close to the ground was I by then. I had just got straight by the time I crossed the threshold but I wasn't pointing the right way - for I was tracking straight at the caravan. Put it down on the runway, lots of right rudder, get it pointing the right way - at last I was safe again.

The full realisation of what had very nearly happened to me hit very hard. I had very nearly written off myself and my aircraft all because of my stupid pride. Of course I should have gone round again, and of course I should not have let thoughts of the ribaldry from my fellow students overcome my better judgement and let me attempt that near fatal crossover.

On that day, pride certainly came before what was very nearly a very bad fall and I have never forgotten the lesson it taught me.

A LUCKY HAND

DH 115 Vampire T11

It was one of those foul days at Sylt when the weather 'Meatbox' had done the round of all the ranges, and no-where was fit for air-to-air. Most of us were settled in the Squadron for a serious game of 'clag', and there was I, with the best hand of the morning. Suddenly, the Boss sticks his head in and says: "Away to Station Flight, horse, and collect the Vampire TXI which they've just mended. Bring it back and don't bend it".

With those cautionary words he withdrew and, with a muttered curse, I donated my fistful to the Squadron Armament Officer, unconvinced that he would preserve my stake. I rushed downstairs and hitched a lift through the mist to Station Flight, miles away on the other side of the airfield. I signed the Form 700, grabbed a start-crew, conducted a somewhat cursory pre-flight check - well, I wasn't going flying, was I?

With my hat on, I signalled for start, and wound-up the old Goblin. I called the Tower for permission to taxy to the Squadron dispersal, and they replied, "Can't see you, horse: call crossing the runway". I waved chocks away, poked on the power, and was soon shifting most satisfactorily on this down-slope. Having checked the brakes and applied rudder to turn right, I presumed that I would soon be back in the game!

Wrong!!! Straight ahead was where this Vampire was going, heading relentlessly towards the standby SAR Whirlwind helicopter dead ahead! I sneaked a quick look at the brake-gauge - it read zero. Distressing visions of an imminent court-martial provoked an even quicker closure of the HP cock, followed by a rapid leap over the side (I wasn't strapped-in, you see) to grab the wing-tip. Thoughtful assistance from the startled groundcrew enabled me to slew the aeroplane round and miss the chopper, although it was a very close call.

That minor event took place in the 1950s and I still remember it well. I learnt a few things from that, I can tell you, and I never got another hand as lucky - not even at 'clag'.

GW

DISORIENTATION

We were on the 'night shift' of a 2-day Station 'Mineval' and programmed to fly 1v2 and 2v2 night tactic sorties. As usual, everything was time critical. The first sortie was uneventful, but delayed 30 minutes due to an practice air raid. The result was that eating, briefing and walking for the second sortie all seemed to happen at once. We were all experienced crews though, we had our roles and aims, knew our sanctuary levels, had done it before, so no problem. Or so we thought!

Various problems ensued on start-up for all bar one aircraft, resulting in Nos 3 and 4 getting airborne first with ourselves as No 2 following 5 minutes later. We contacted our SOC and 'the fights on' (l v 2) was called as we coasted out.

The weather was poor, but suitable. It was IMC from below 2000 ft to around 10,000 ft with cloud layers above that in places. The threat was 2 'Fulcrums' both Fox 1 capable.

We had both contact from about 40 nms, at 35nms they split and we decided to press the northerly contact, who eventually ran out leaving us 5 nms in his six o'clock. From GCI it was apparent we were being dragged into the other 'Fulcrum' and we so pumped, leaving us at 3000 ft with a 'Fulcrum' 5 miles behind us and the other no factor. We ran the entire length of the area at 570 kts but we were unable to gain further separation; with land fast approaching we decided to turn back.

Our plan was initially to climb to the medium block, but as I pitched the nose 30º up, the speed immediately reduced to around 500 kts due to the 1500 litre tank fit and heavy fuel weight. I selected reheat, but it soon became apparent that we could not safely transit the opposition's 8000-12,000 ft sanctuary block, so we opted to level at 7000 ft. At around 5000 ft I deselected reheat and rolled the aircraft to the right to allow the nose to drop. As we levelled at 7600 ft I pulled and overbanked by 10° to get back to below 7000 ft. Shortly after stabilising in this attitude the HUD began to 'ladder', the pitch altitude lines seeming to rise up the display and then jump back to where they started. This fixed my attention fully on the HUD, the Nav was 'heads in' looking at the radar for the bogey and he called a second or two later that he had an inertial navigation platform problem; sure enough, the HUD symbology then disappeared completely. Immediately, I was totally disorientated and referred to the 'head down' AI - expecting indications of a 90° banked right hand turn. Whilst the brain registered horror and confusion at 'lots of nose down', instinctive reaction took over.

The video showed I immediately rolled the wings level the correct way and began to pull. I clearly remember 45° nose down passing 4000 ft at approximately 450 kts. The brain had recovered by now and I called "g coming on" which thankfully the Nav took to mean I'd regained control. I opted for a controlled pull out rather than a 'snatched' high-g gut reaction. Five and a half g produced a satisfactory pitch rate and we bottomed out at 1500 ft AMSL. A shaky 'knock it off' was called and we decided to recover to base due to our nervous disposition and the marginal overstress of the 1500 litre tanks, which still contained fuel.

As we were close to base we decided to dump fuel from 5800 kg to 2000 kg; dumping started normally: hand on the switches, pre-descent/recovery checks complete, correct recovery time, etc. Hang on, why am I flying left handed? Switch the fuel dumps off - only 1500 kg left! This definitely wasn't funny any more. Everything was done from the FRCs verbatim from then on, until I was safely standing outside the aircraft - scared, but much wiser!

Panavia Tornado F3

What are the learning points from this incident?

I remember on the OCU being told to cross-reference the HUD with the primary attitude indicator head down. If the HUD plays up, go 'heads-in' earlier not later. In fast jets, if something goes wrong, by their very nature it happens fast. The entire manoeuvre and recovery took just 15 seconds. Having survived a frightening incident, think forwards all the time, never about what has just happened, you may distract yourself and cause more problems - as I nearly did. To that end, check and double check everything. Finally, in the initial climb and subsequent pull, we were trying to defeat an adversary with an aggressive manoeuvre, which we did, but in so doing we could have flown into the sea. Night and IMC manoeuvres must be tempered to account for the ground having a kill probability of 1, in both real and training scenarios. Live missiles and training rounds never have the same probability of success.

SMOKE ON......GO!

I was one of the fortunate members of a fairly well known establishment who did his flying training at the nearby satellite airfield perched on top of one of Lincolnshire's four hills. On two or three half-days each week, we would make a break from the rigours of cadet life to sample the reality of the world outside,

On one such day, I was due to undertake a solo cross country exercise. One of my friends was set to go on the same exercise some 10 minutes before me and we had made secret plans to indulge in a little illicit formation flying. Details were soon confirmed: check in on 282.8 (our private 'quiet' frequency) after setting heading on the first leg, join up as soon as possible thereafter, and away into the wide blue yonder!

The first aircraft I was allocated was unserviceable and so I looked like being more than 20 minutes behind my 'playmate'. I jumped into my second JP and hastily flashed through the checks, started up and belted round the taxyway to the end of Runway 36. I pushed the throttle forward, released the brakes and trundled away. As soon as I was airborne, I thumped the undercarriage button and heard the satisfying clunk of the wheels coming up. Almost immediately, the cockpit filled with smoke. God, what's happened? I flicked on 100% cent oxygen, made a panic call to ATC, turned crosswind and meanwhile decided that the nosewheel had come up off-centre, causing the tyre to rub away in the well. Lowering the undercarriage stopped the smoke. Brilliant diagnosis, but how will she behave on the ground? By this time, the Duty Instructor had the glasses on me and said that there appeared to be nothing wrong with the nosewheel, but I was far from convinced; after all, the smoke had stopped when I lowered the undercarriage! I suddenly realised I was frightened.

The ensuing landing was quite uneventful, but I shut down as soon as I had cleared the runway and waited for my instructor who was careering round the perimeter track in a Land Rover. Feelings of pleasure at my superb handling of the situation and my relief at being in one piece vanished soon after he leapt up on the wing root. He noticed almost immediately that I had not selected the rain/ice clearance lever to 'off' and had burned out the system!

I should have learned about flying from that, but didn't! I went on to have my illicit formation trip on another cross country and so now I'm a Secretarial Officer!

CG

ONE FOR THE LOG BOOK

LC

In the early 1960s, life in the RAF was somewhat less regimented than it is now. There was a good deal more 'freedom of the individual', which often produced an attrition rate that became unsustainable in the later years of increasing budget restraints.

It was early morning at a Royal Air Force Flying Training School 'somewhere in England'. The daily ritual of the Met Briefing had just finished and the Chief Instructor had called for an airborne weather check before committing himself to the programme for the day. This was the open invitation beloved by most young instructors. It had become traditional that the first instructor airborne gave the weather check details over the radio and the short flight invariably started and finished with a 'beat-up' of the airfield. This practice had become highly competitive with each instructor trying to outdo his predecessor.

The man of the moment eased the Jet Provost into a gentle climbing turn to gain speed, picked a line that would take him across the airfield at an angle to the runway in use and pass close by the control tower in full view of the slower 'met briefers' who were, even then, making their leisurely way to the flights.

We shall be charitable and assume that the Instructor's pre-flight check had been conducted in more than the usual haste. He had not noticed that his aircraft had been fuelled to full tip-tanks. Now the JP Mk 3 was not noted for its sparkling performance - indeed, it was unkindly known as the 'constant thrust, variable noise machine' and the performance of a fully-fuelled Mk 3 verged on the abysmal.

As the aircraft crossed the main runway, the Instructor pulled up the nose, applied full nose-down trim and rolled inverted, resulting in a truly spectacular 'beat-up'. The 'beat-up' was certainly spectacular. The aircraft screeched over the visibly impressed audience with the brave instructor waving cheerily as he eased around the control tower. It started to climb gently as the Instructor attempted to roll back to the more normal upright attitude but, ultimately, this was too much for the poor Jet Provost. Although giving all of its 1750 lbs of thrust, it had been forced to drag itself inverted over the airfield, had its nose pushed high up into the air and then was invited to roll with the application of full aileron.

The airspeed and the pilot's ideas both gave out at about the same time. As the aircraft sank towards a line of poplar trees on the airfield boundary, shocked controllers in the Tower heard the pilot's last words over the radio, and they were recorded for posterity.

"TIMBER-R-R-R".

Miraculously, the pilot survived. The Jet Provost and some of the poplars did not. Being back in the 'good old days', the Instructor was court-martialled, had his career prospects interfered with, and was sent to a job where he would exert far less influence on impressionable young minds.

Shortly afterwards, Flying Training Command (as it then was) produced an order dealing with the conduct of airborne weather checks. Nobody was too surprised!

TOO TYRED TO FLY - PROPERLY?

Way back in the early 1970s, I was Deputy Chief Flying Instructor (DCFI) at a Royal Air Force regional gliding club somewhere in Oxfordshire. It was a small club but on which prided itself on its friendly atmosphere, its general performance and, most of all, its unrivalled safety record. There were at the time two DCFIs at our club - one was responsible for Advanced Instruction and the other (namely me) had responsibility for Basic Training up to and including first solo. Any instructor worth his salt will know you are seldom able to relax when actually teaching. In fact, it is fair to say I had only been frightened once up until I gained my instructor's certificate, but from then on I reckon I was frightened at least once on every trip! One could, therefore, only properly relax between trips.

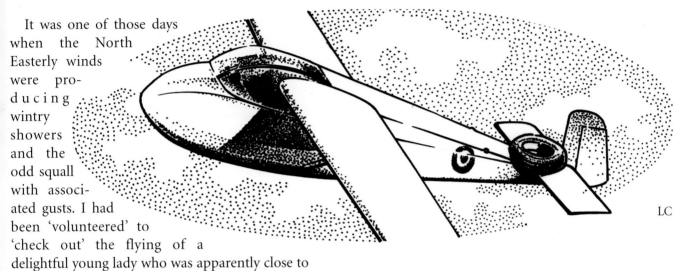

It was one of those days when the North Easterly winds were producing wintry showers and the odd squall with associated gusts. I had been 'volunteered' to 'check out' the flying of a delightful young lady who was apparently close to going solo. This, of course, I was pleased to do, as an instructor's perks included assisting the said lovely lady to strap in. With a beautiful smile, she informed me she had been having a little trouble with her speed control, having to use unusual forward stick pressure to maintain certain set speeds.

LC

The glider that we were about to fly, a Ka 4, had the most rudimentary trim system known to man. A large spring placed a direct load on the stick and it was adjusted (if you were very quick) by a compression wheel on top. Adjustment would usually take most of the four-minute circuit time available! With this in mind, I cleverly suggested that the young lady may wish to take a little more ballast into the front cockpit than she normally did in order to bring her further into the weight band allowed. This would have the effect of altering the centre of gravity and lowering the nose, thus unloading the stick. She therefore grabbed an extra 20 lbs of ballast and we strapped in.

The circuit was planned to be straightforward with me just observing her performance, hopefully preparing her to go solo within the next few trips. Then there was a delay - the winch was giving problems; we waited for the cable for some time until a line squall forming upwind meant we had to 'stack' until it had blown through. So, we got out and moved the glider crosswind to the lee of the old bus that we used as a canteen. We carefully picketed the glider, placed old car tyres on the wingtip and tailplane and retired into the bus for a cup of tea whilst the squall blew through. All the other club members were inside, plus the CFI, the second DCFI and several other instructors. The talk degenerated to its normal levels of summer thermals, beer and sex (not necessarily in that order). In short, the instructors were relaxing!

The squall eventually cleared. The CFI shouted that we needed to get launched quickly because another shower was already building upwind. Nobody argued with our CFI; we all did what Jock said! Two DCFIs, the CFI and at least two other instructors pushed the Ka 4 on line, the delightful young lady and I strapped in, the cable arrived, we hitched on, checked all clear 'above and behind', gave the commands 'Up slack!' and 'All out!' and got airborne.

It was then that it all went to worms! The glider's nose pitched up in excess of 45°! My God, I thought, she does have problems with speed control! In a slightly strangled tone, I suggested (forcefully) that she should reduce the angle of climb. I didn't quite catch the response, but I now suspect it was probably something to the effect that she was unable to change the attitude! Anyway, the speed was within limits and, luckily, the launch continued to about 800 ft. We released and the speed rapidly decayed to about 2 kts above the stall. As it had now gone awfully quiet due to the low speed, I calmly suggested that we could do with about 5 kts more for a comfortable flight. Nothing happened! I repeated my request and was told in no uncertain terms by the now non-smiling young lady that she was unable to comply! I took control for the first time in the flight only to discover that the stick was fully forward! With the speed just above the stall, I wound the trim wheel fully to the nose down position - the speed still remained just above the stall! At this point, I ran out of ideas.

I now needed to concentrate on the impending landing. In the interests of safety it was normal practice to increase the speed on base leg prior to the final turn. The total required increase over the normal flying speed on that particular day had been calculated at approximately 18 kts! We were, apparently, about 22 kts (give or take a few) short of the correct landing speed! In consequence, all turns from that point on were made very, very carefully and very, very gently.

The approach and landing seemed to take forever. Ground speed was minimal, as could be expected, and both of us in the glider were very conscious of the next line squall, with its associated gusts and wind shear, advancing rapidly down the field. We eventually touched down, undershooting the normal stopping point by about 30 yds. Most embarrassing to the ego but at least we came to a halt in an undamaged condition!

At this point, I became aware of several people running towards us from the bus. One of them, on arrival at the glider, asked me if we'd noticed anything wrong about the flight. I started to mutter something uncomplimentary about student speed control when I noticed he was pointing at our tailplane. I unstrapped, lifted the canopy and got out. There, on the tailplane, wedged firmly against the base of the fin, was a well worn radial tyre weighing about 15 lbs!

That day I learnt about flying, and how you can never afford to relax; how it's never advisable to fly close to centre of gravity limits; how supervision can break down even in the best of establishments; how you should never rush pre-flight checks; and how adrenaline is brown. The young lady? She kept very quiet, listened, took it all completely in her stride and went solo that evening - without a tyre on the tail!

SOME LESSONS ARE LEARNT THE HARD WAY

Hunting Jet Provost

I was a B1 creamed off QFI in the early 1960s at No 3 FTS, which was then based at RAF Leeming. I had taken one of my students across to RAF Topcliffe for circuit consolidation. After checking him out during the transit to Topcliffe, I sent him solo for an hour in the circuit. Whilst he was airborne, I was told to plan on refuelling the aircraft at Topcliffe when he had completed his sortie, before returning to Leeming to carry out a running change with another student who I was to take on his 'Mid-Basic Test' - his end of circuit phase check.

All went to plan and, whilst the new student was strapping in, I briefed him on the test and on what I expected of him. We taxied out and took off. As he raised the flaps (at about 110 kts I seem to remember), I closed the throttle to practise an engine failure after take-off (EFATO). Turnback speed for the JP Mk 3 was over 150 kts and so all I was looking for was a statement to the effect that we were too slow to turn-

back, an indication that there was no suitable place to force-land, and so we would have to eject. Instead, I got a 3g turn to the right, back towards the airfield. Very quickly we stalled in the turn, whereupon I took over, levelled the wings and opened the throttle whilst pointing out in my best QFI manner that he had not done the correct drill. Regrettably, the engine didn't respond, the speed was about 70 kts and the height must have been about 100 - 200 ft. This was not the healthiest of situations, for the Martin Baker seat then in the JP3 had minimum ejection limits of around 200 ft and 120 kts.

Those who know Leeming may recall that if you take off on the Northerly runway and then turn right you end up over Scruton Wood - there was nowhere to force land and so I ordered an ejection and jettisoned the canopy. Meanwhile, I was attempting a relight and sending out a Mayday. I then let go of the stick and grabbed the top ejection handle. The stalled aircraft pitched down and my seat fired, with scarcely enough time for the drogue chute to deploy before I hit a tree.

My student died as result of his injuries. His parachute had managed to open, but he hit a fence and was then struck by either the canopy or my ejection seat. I survived with lots of broken bones. As I lay in Nocton Hall Hospital completely paralysed from the neck down apart from some movement in my left arm, one of the first letters to reach me was from Jimmy Martin of Martin Baker congratulating me on a successful ejection. I spent most of 1963 in Nocton Hall and Headley Court but was back flying within a year.

The engine had apparently failed because a fault in the fuel control unit had prevented fuel going to the collector tank from the moment we opened the throttle for take off. In effect, we got airborne with only the two-gallon contents of the collector tank and these were exhausted at about the time I closed the throttle for the practice!

What did I learn from this incident?

✈ Good briefings are not given in a rush, on the flight line, whilst the other participant is concentrating on something else such as strapping in, loading the INAS or tuning the radios.

✈ As far as I am aware, EFATO turnback drills have never saved anybody, yet several people have been killed and injured whilst practising them. I have since always argued against turnbacks!

✈ I apparently had no more than 8 - 10 seconds (it seemed like longer) from realising that I had a problem to hitting the tree.

✈ The engine could not have been relit in that time and so (with hind sight) I realise I wasted precious seconds attempting to do so.

✈ The ejection was in full view of ATC and half of RAF Leeming so I could have saved time on the Mayday.

✈ In those days, the seat pan handle was considered the secondary handle. However, in my situation, I didn't need face protection and use of the seat pan handle may have saved another few milliseconds.

LC

PROBABLY THE BEST FUEL LEAK IN THE WORLD

The year was 1955 and it was one of those awful claggy weather situations which were so common at Sylt in late Autumn. The weather had been solidly clamped for a week - cloudbase about six feet, visibility half a mile and, to put it mildly if not bitterly, the chaps were getting a bit brassed off. In fact the only bit of inno-

Venom FB4

cent merriment to brighten an otherwise tedious detachment had been afforded by the OC Flying who had taken off a week earlier on a weather recce, and was still cooling his heels at Schleswig-land. Each morning, we would all troop dutifully off to Met briefing to gaze earnestly at the one isobar draped across Northern Europe, which showed no signs of moving. Each morning, we would listen with no great enthusiasm to the fractured tones of our German forecaster as he jubilantly prognosticated yet another day of 'fock und low straytus'. Each morning, we would mooch aimlessly off to the flights past the rows of silently dripping Venoms and brace ourselves for yet another hilarious day of cards, coffee and aircraft recognition slides.

However, one bright spot looming on the otherwise dull horizon was a cocktail party which we were throwing for the station staff on the Friday, before flying back to base on the Saturday. This promised to be a thrunge of no mean dimensions as national honour was involved, Belgian and Danish squadrons also being represented. And so it proved. Conversation was difficult above the deafening clicks of brain master switches being turned off. Dinner time came and went and lo! no food was consumed. The bar was closed at its usual time, but not quite quickly enough to prevent the purchase of five or six crates of Carlsberg; and those whose livers survived a tour in 2ATAF will remember that a crate of Carlsberg contained 60 bottles.... Songs were sung, jokes were exchanged, lines were shot, the inscrutable was unscrewed, and all in all it was a night to remember, which was a pity, as nobody could remember it subsequently; not very clearly, anyway. We weren't bothered though. Clampers chaps - no flying tomorrow - not to worry.

The next morning, my first semiconscious impression was of a shaft of bright light striking me firmly between the eyes as my godly, righteous and sickeningly sober roommate pulled the curtains. I was in my own bed, which surprised me. At first, I thought I was going to die and then, as consciousness returned, I became afraid that I might live. I sat up, fell over, tottered out for a quick technicolour yawn, and came back to check on the situation. Disaster! Sunshine and blue sky! One thing was certain, I was not in a fit state to carry out anything except shallow respiration that day. A Carlsberg hangover was a fearsome thing at the best of times, and I had one which was the Grade A, King-size, deckle-edge, family economy pack granddaddy of them all.

I sat through the briefing for the return flight clutching the sides of my chair and fighting off waves of nausea. I signed the Authorisation Book and Form 700 with both hands and wobbled out to find my aircraft.

Please let it be unserviceable. Please don't let me fly. Please . . . Silent prayers fled upwards, faltered, and thudded to the ground again exhausted. I shook the tip tanks hoping they'd drop off. I kicked the tyres hoping they'd go down. I searched the aircraft for the slightest reason for putting it unserviceable - and then I saw it! Drip. Drip. Drip. Fuel oozing from underneath. With a strangled grunt, I called over the Fitter.

"Venting, Sir. They were filled up last night and the sun's expanding the fuel and it's venting".
"Never mind (hic) I wannit checked!"
I could see the little balloon creep out of his ear with 'Thinks: Drunken bum!' written on it but I didn't care.
The Corporal came over. "Anything wrong, Sir?"
"Yes... Fuel leak".
"No, it's venting, Sir. They were filled up last night and the sun..."
"I know! But I still wannit checked (hic)".

Yet another little balloon with writing on it. And another one (bigger, stronger and dirtier) when the Chief came over. But I didn't care. Anything, any excuse would do. Reproachfully, they got a screwdriver. Silently, they unscrewed the engine cover. Slowly, they removed it. Sneeringly, they looked up - and saw a dirty great crack in the main fuel tank from which fuel was dripping onto the engine .

And the moral of that story is, don't get smashed before going flying 'cos your fuel tank may not have a leak in it! (Alternatively: Don't get smashed before going flying without having a leak first!)

DO YOU SEE WHAT I SEE?

As an Air Defender, I am quite convinced about the two-crew concept. At the least there is an extra pair of eyes checking your tail as you shoot down yet another F-15 on the ACMI. At the best, there is that immensely satisfying feeling of working a complicated intercept to the best combination of tactics and weapons parameters. However, it can go wrong and I would now like to relate one of those times.

Fortunately, it was not whilst I was on an air defence squadron; I was doing a tour as a test pilot at Boscombe Down. A large part of the job entailed flying photo-chase sorties to record weapons releases and one of

Sea Eagle Missile

those weapons was Sea Eagle. The job was easy, on the face of it. Take film of the Sea Eagle in flight to check that the systems were working as advertised. As usual, there was a slight glitch. To ensure an accurate recording, we had to be fairly close to the beast, which meant very low and very fast.

Several crews had a go at the task and found it too much. Then it was my turn. The photographer and I had worked together before, so each of us knew something of how the other guy functioned. Our planning was meticulous. A Sea Eagle was put on a plinth outside the Squadron whilst I looked at it from various angles to make sure I knew the best aspect to ensure the photographer got the shots he wanted, and we also spent some time discussing how to get into formation with the missile.

Our plan was simple. The next launch was to be a salvo of two so I would accelerate as the first missile dropped, hoping to pick up the second. As it transpired, it worked perfectly; come the day, I fell neatly into position on the second missile. The aspect was correct, the distance was right and the speed was spot on. "There you are, mate", I said, "film away".

"OK", came the response, "but you are too far away". No problem, ease in and down a bit. "How's that?"

"Better, but still too far away." I must have got that aspect completely wrong. Never mind - go for it. "Still too far." By this time we were some way down range and I was nearly flying echelon with the thing. "Andy, (the photographer's name) mate. Even amongst the boys this is getting a bit hairy." "What do you Mean? . . . Aargh!!"

You've guessed it. Andy was filming the first missile and I was formating on the second. Their aspect was such that every time (as the film showed) I moved the aircraft to his commands, the exact thing he wanted happened. However, until he screamed, the field of view of the camera was too narrow for him to pick up the second missile.

Why did he scream? Oh that's easy. He screamed because the view of the missile that he thought we were formating on, and which he was filming, was suddenly blocked by a very large row of rivets as the second (and much nearer) missile came into shot.

So, when you're flying your aircraft on the ACMI are you really sure that your nav/pilot is looking at the same F-15 as you are?

TO HILL...AND BACK...

It was the summer of 1980 and I was doing a recce course in England on a fast jet (with nozzles). I was flying a solo recce mission and had just completed my first target, a linesearch. I was then transiting towards my second target, following a route over the Pennines. Since the workload was low, I decided to ring the areas on the map that I had photographed as likely targets. The weather was good and the horizon excellent. The aircraft felt trimmed and I eased it up to about 400 ft AGL. I started to ring the likely areas and note what I had seen. I was aware of the dangers of head-in-the-cockpit, low-level flying but after checking it was clear ahead a couple of times whilst writing, everything looked OK and I continued with my notes. Then, suddenly, a 'bell' rang in my brain to say I had overstepped my 'head-in' time.

I'm not sure why it rang; I guess it was probably that mixture of experience and self-preservation that most pilots develop. Anyway, I'm glad it did, because as I looked up I saw a hill. It wasn't a little hill or a big one safely off to one side; it completely filled the windscreen and extended above the canopy arch.

Instinctively, and very violently, I pulled the control column back until it hit the rear stop. Unfortunately, all that happened was that the aircraft started to go into wing rock and deep buffet and the flight path remained the same, so the hill just got closer. Just as quickly and violently, I smashed the control column forward against the front stop to clear the deep buffet - it felt like I was going to push it through the INAS map. Again just as quickly, I pulled the control column back but stopped it as I felt light buffet. How long those three movements took to complete I'm not sure; my guess is that it was PDQ. (I didn't take any nozzles or put on full power - my left arm was frozen in fear).

The hill was by now very close and I was stuck deep in 'coffin corner' - pull any more and I'd lose the lift, pull any less and I'd hit the hill. The nose started to rise and the ground got closer. Just before the 'moment critique', the nose broke the horizon and the hill slope flashed past my cockpit at about head height. For those of you who have flown very close to the ground, you may know that sensation where every boulder becomes sharply defined. So that was it; I'd missed by about 30 ft, maybe less.

I levelled at 2000 ft AGL and had a quick think. I could either chuck in low flying there and then or learn my lesson, go back to low level and continue. In the end, I returned to low level, albeit very chastened by my experience.

The lesson is an old one but I hope you can learn from it without having to go through that slow motion film that will always live with me. Low-level is a dangerous environment at any time, so if you must go 'inside' the cockpit for whatever reason, take it in stages, keep those stages very short and spend lots of time looking out in between. Looking in nearly killed me, but I was lucky - no sheep got in the way!

GW

DIVINE INTERVENTION

Way back in the dark ages of early Vampire Squadron days, a mighty beast was delivered to our Squadron. It was called a Meteor 7. As frightening tales were soon being whispered about this monster (including the fact that it had two engines!), it was pushed into the farthest and darkest corner of the hangar and we all tried very hard to forget all about it. However, it just wouldn't go away and it eventually appeared all shining and bright on the ASP alongside our cowering little Vampires, leaving us no choice but to fly it. Alarming tales were told of first solos and no one went short of advice, but it's worth remembering that this occurred in those rather pleasant days when one read a very slim volume of Pilot's Notes before the Flight Commander gave you a thorough oral test by asking you what the landing speed was. Then off you went!

Being a two-seater, it was naturally used occasionally to carry two pilots from A to B, and it was on one such occasion that my tale really begins. The Squadron were going, en masse, to a funeral and I was slotted in the rear seat of the Meteor. The chap in front was flying it and, as we both had a grand total of about 90 minutes in Meteors, neither of us was particularly brimming with confidence in the ability of the other to land the monster. However, we arrived in the circuit at our destination and my 'Captain' began his approach to land. Those familiar with early Meteor 7s will know what I mean when I say that at the beginning of the final turn I saw the flap lever moving up and down like a yo-yo as the operator tried to find the central position to lock the flaps at the quarter setting. Realising what was going on and having had similar difficulty myself, I said "OK . . . I'll put it down", to which he answered "Ta". My solicitousness was, of course, principally motivated by a desire for him to devote all his attention to landing, since this held out the best prospect of us both walking away afterwards.

LC

The aircraft continued on a gentle curve of pursuit towards the runway, began to roll out just before contact and then struck the ground with a sickening thud. The damage was not too bad considering, but looking back, it should really have been an unexplained double fatal.

I've no doubt you have all guessed by now. Yes, the aircraft landed unaided by either of us! My "I'll put it down" was taken, with a sigh of relief, by the man up front to mean that I realised I was so clever that I was going to land it from the back. Naturally, I meant only that I would put the flap down.

A few years later, I became a Qualified Flying Instructor on the same type of aircraft and was probably the most insistent man in the entire Command for saying, "I have control", and hearing clearly back, "You have control". I definitely learnt about flying from that.

SAY WHAT YOU MEAN AND...

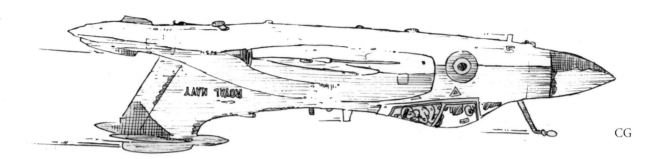

CG

Some years ago I had the good fortune to fly Buccaneers with the Royal Navy during a tour embarked on a venerable aircraft carrier. The Mk 2 version of the Buccaneer was very new in those days. In fact, our Squadron was the first to be equipped with it, and we had to put up with numerous engine modification programmes involving many engine changes - not always an easy task on a carrier. However, at the end of one session when almost every aircraft had undergone another double engine change, our stalwart Squadron Junior Engineer, who was known as Split Pin, was offered a sortie as a reward for all his hard work. It was, naturally, a double engine flight test.

Split Pin was not a keen aviator, but he duly accepted the offer and was eventually strapped into the rear seat of a Buccaneer by a couple of grinning ratings. Not surprisingly he found the accommodation in the rear cockpit rather unpleasant. Meanwhile, I jumped in (you couldn't really do external checks with half the aircraft sticking out over the South China Sea) and started up. Halfway through the after-start checks, a voice from the back seat said "Is it serviceable then?" "Of course not," I retorted, "None of the aircraft you lot service ever are!" I was joking, of course, but unfortunately Split Pin took me literally.

At that point he unstrapped because he was so uncomfortable. He was not surprised when I taxied towards the catapult because the SOP for unserviceable aircraft was to keep their engines running and move forward to park clear of the flight deck landing area. However, he was startled when the aircraft was tensioned up on the catapult. "Hey, what's happening? Are we going to be launched?" he enquired. "Of course!" said I, busying myself with the engine checks before launch. I didn't know that Split Pin was unstrapped and he hadn't dared to tell me!

Anyway, off we went, and I flew the whole flight test profile, chanting out all the important figures to a strangely silent passenger. Eventually we recovered back on board without incident and it was only after shutting down that I discovered that Split Pin had spent the whole sortie trying to strap himself in again. Needless to say, his attempts weren't very successful, nor had he taken down any of the readings required by the flight test schedule!

The lessons of this sad story are: firstly, always say what you really mean when you are in an aircraft and, secondly, never joke with engineers about the serviceability of their aircraft - they always take it too seriously.

HS Buccaneer S2

EJECT IN TIME

As I near the end of my 12-year SSC, my mind has been drifting back more and more to my early days in flying training. Despite the fact that I have been flying helicopters since 1987, whenever there is a fast jet fatality which has resulted from a pilot not ejecting in time I recall an April day when I might so easily have become another in a long line of statistics.

The entry in my log book looks innocent enough:

'Apr 24 JP5A XW408 Self Solo Ex 76. GH. Including interesting stall turn. 1 Hr'.

But was it? Well, you see, it was like this...

Some 18 of us had started BFT almost a year earlier. Air-sickness claimed one victim early on, spin aeros test accounted for another, and AIFG a third. By the time we approached the BHT, we were down to 15 and, with no multi-engine training slots available, it was fast jet, helicopters, or bust. In short, the pressure was on (as always) and the one thing we had sussed out pretty early on was that 'He who cocks up gets chopped!'

For the lucky few who had not encountered problems somewhere along the line, BHT was 'just another check ride', but for those of us who had struggled / were struggling / might struggle in the future, it was a major watershed. Essentially, it was make or break, and at that time there were still a lot of back seats in the Tornado force that needed filling if the CFI thought that was where your destiny lay.

Anyway, one day, after a competent enough dual check ride, I was sent off to practise my aeros sequence. There was just one caveat "Don't pratt around at 15,000 ft, do your aeros as low as you can, to get the best performance out of the jet. That's what the examiner will be looking for next week". So off I went, outbound from Cranwell, turn left at the A1, climb to a sensible height, throw a quick set of HASELLs in and off we go.

Now I hope former JP instructors will excuse me for what might be a slip of the mind, but although it was nine years ago, I still have the following numbers in my mind. My base height on this day was, I think, FL90 and I believe stall turns, loops, and the like took about 2000 ft to get to the top of the manoeuvre. Similarly, I also seem to remember that spinning (dual only of course) was always commenced above 15,000 ft.

As I pulled up for my first loop, spin entry height did not really seem too important. In fact, all was still going well until I fell out of the recovery from a stall turn. Not 'fell out' so much, but instead of the instructor's crisp recovery, the aircraft seemed to be behaving more like a pendulum on the way down. "Don't be shy, stop the aircraft swinging with rudder", I recalled him saying from the dual trip. Right. One bootfull of right pedal was duly applied and.. bloody hell, it didn't do that before!

By now, the 'razor sharp' brain that had seconds earlier diagnosed a scrappy stall turn recovery, was informing me (surprisingly calmly, funnily enough) that I had entered a spin. This was not so good for I was definitely not authorised for spinning! Never mind, follow the drill: "Centralise the controls within the first turn of the spin and the aircraft will recover immediately". Every student knew this to be the case, it was elementary and beyond debate.

Hmm. That's strange. I have definitely centralised the controls but the aircraft is still spinning. There's definitely something fishy going on. What's more, it isn't just spinning, it's going faster than I have ever seen it go in practice. Worse still, I can't even see the sun to count the turns of spin... I have no idea how long these thoughts took. I have no idea how high, or perhaps more importantly, how low I was. I just knew that I had done exactly as instructed, ie centralised the controls, and that the trusty JP was not acting as advertised. This was disconcerting to say the very least.

Then all of a sudden, an instructor's voice came back to me from ground school almost a year earlier: "If you find yourself in an unusual spin when all you can see in the canopy is the earth, you are hanging in your straps and there is buffet on the control column, then you will be in an inverted spin, and I do believe that the JP is so stable, that all you have to do is ease the stick back a fraction until the buffet stops and the aircraft will then fly out". I saw the light. The symptoms were all there; buffet, lack of sky, strap ends dangling in front of my nose. I eased back on the stick and, sure enough, the aircraft flew out. Admittedly, it did leave me in a fairly unusual position, but it was definitely flying again. The UP recovery did go as planned and in no time at all I had traded speed (a lot of it) for height, and was straight and level again with cruise power selected. Time for some checks.

Right. Location? Instruments erect, enough fuel to get home, altimeters cross-checked at FL60. FL60? What the hell am I doing down here? Not only was I below my aeros base height, but I realised then that I had also gone through my minimum (spin) abandonment height and not even realised it. Not so good.

Later that evening, I eventually plucked up the courage to confess my sins to my instructor in 'Happy Hour'. Far from the slapping I was expecting, he just chuckled and asked why I thought we were taught spin recoveries in the first place. A good point that and one I had missed. But what about the moral of the story?

Well, I was flying the aircraft and I wasn't distracted because I did (eventually) diagnose and deal with the problem. However, I was far more concerned about performing an illegal and unauthorised exercise than I was about saving my neck, and I had certainly failed to monitor the height which was my greatest error without a doubt.

So, if you are a student approaching BHT (*or anyone else .... says Spry*) and you find yourself in the unfortunate position of being in an unplanned spin, my advice to you would be "Check height" and if necessary, opt for the Martin Baker let-down.

BAC Jet Provost T5A

TOO CLOSE FOR COMFORT

I was on detachment at Bodo in Norway while flying F-4 Phantoms in the late 1970s. The weather had been dismal throughout our stay and we were flying 'Delta fit' because of the stiff diversion requirements; for those who aren't familiar with the Phantom, 'Delta fit' meant three tanks and a rather sluggish jet.

One day, our Norwegian hosts had some visitors and we were asked if a four-ship we had planned could overfly

McDonnell Douglas F-4 Phantom

the Squadron buildings after take-off as a sort-of ad hoc flypast. We discussed it and decided the simplest plot would be to jink right through about 20° immediately after take-off as the overfly site was offset to the right at the far end of the active runway. The crosswind was from the right and so line-up would be in echelon starboard. Because of the line-up and the need to jink right, we briefed a safe 30-second stream departure.

As we taxied out we were warned that a SAS airliner was inbound and advised that we might have to hold. Bodo is a joint military/civil airfield and this was quite a regular occurrence. The decision on whether or not we had to hold was actually borderline under the Norwegian rules which applied and so the Norwegian air traffic controller asked us if we could expedite. As we knew our F-104 adversaries were already airborne, we agreed. The crosswind was too brisk for pairs take-offs and so the leader called for rolling singleton take-offs and fastest stream. We all acknowledged and I assumed (an assumption that I learned later was shared by the others) that the immediate jink on take-off was either delayed or binned. Anyway, as number two in the stream, I decided that I would just follow my leader.

We rocked those babies outboard, hit the heaters and went for it. Lead took the hard left side of the runway and I took middle left. The leader rotated. I rotated. Just then the leader held it down, jinked right and I was presented with wall-to-wall F-4 in my front screen while I was struggling to pull the jet airborne. A fully-fuelled Delta fit F-4 is not the happiest of jets just after rotate and just as I was thinking 'it's a funny old game', I hit his jetwash. Having had the front F-4 pass in front by feet rather than yards and having nearly collected the leader's 50,000 lb plus aircraft, I felt privileged. A nanosecond later I was out the other side, still alive and going for the flypast with my hair on fire. In the brief difficult moment beforehand I exhaustively examined all the corners of the F-4-not-crashing envelope as the AOA gauge registered obscene positives and negatives, the yaw ball bounced off the stops in both directions and I thrashed the control stick to a blurred frenzy.

It was an interesting debrief. The leader accepted the flak, but asked why none of us had prompted him to clarify the timing of the jink with the reduced stream time. To a man, we said we had assumed a delayed jink - and, anyway, it was not considered manly to witter on the radio at a foreign airfield. What did I learn in coming so close to buying the farm? First, don't assume - check. Second, if you change the brief do make sure that everybody understands the change.

Oh, by the way, we won the fight - and the Norwegians thought the flypast was just great!

ALL AT SEA

CG

ollowing my exchange posting to Canada I was appointed as Squadron Leader Operations at RAF Coltishall in 1972 for the final years of the Lightning there. Unfortunately, the job was not a flying appointment - OC Ops Wg flew and I was left to manage the admin side. However, one distinct prize which went with the job was being in command of the Battle of Britain Flight, so I spent most weekends flying and displaying the aircraft around the UK.

One weekend I was scheduled to do a Hurricane flypast somewhere in the North on a Saturday and then give a full display at East Midlands Airport on the Sunday afternoon. I had also been asked by a station commander in Scotland to bring a Hurricane to the airfield for a display and, if possible, an overnight stop, as he wanted to surprise a terminally-ill Honorary Member of the Officers' Mess who was an ex-Hurricane man.

All started to plan; I did my flypast and then headed on to Scotland for a night stop. The Honorary Member and the Station Commander watched the display and were given a VIP tour of the aircraft, after which I had a most enjoyable evening in the Mess bar. Next morning I discovered that a cold front was situated between me in Scotland and East Midlands Airport. The weather at Coltishall and at East Midlands was good, but somehow I had to get through or under the front if I was to make the show. The crowd expected the Hurricane, and the organisers knew that the weather at my base and at their airport was within limits for a show.

I elected to head south and hope that I could remain in contact with the ground by flying below the front. The instruments in the Hurricane were not up to serious instrument flying, and neither was I as I didn't have a current rating. As I approached the front and the Yorkshire Moors, I decided my best bet was to head out to sea, the height of which I knew and where I should be able to get below the weather. It worked. I arrived at the show on time, gave my display and then headed home to Coltishall, but I never did anything like that ever again.

I had ended up over the sea, with no life saving jacket or dinghy, skimming the wave tops with little forward visibility and with rain pouring into the cockpit and running down the instrument panel. I was both frightened and cross that I had allowed myself to get into such a pickle.

The moral? Be careful when you think that your heart is ruling your head.

Hawker Hurricane

A WOLF IN SHEEPSKIN

In 1970, as a mature non-volunteer who had been dragged kicking and screaming to Little Rissington, I graduated from Central Flying School with a shiny B2 on Chipmunks. Yorkshire Universities Air Squadron was already on Summer Camp at RAF Abingdon and I joined them there to complete the Camp before moving with the rest of the Unit to home base at Church Fenton.

My acceptance check was conducted by the 'Boss' on the first day and I was duly let loose on my first students, most of whom actually had more Chipmunk experience than I. On the Tuesday of my second week, I was selected to fly with OC Ops Wg over the lunch period whilst the UAS Instructors repaired to the Mess for lunch.

LC

The 'Wing Commander student' duly arrived. He was dressed to fly and explained that he had been lucky enough to be allocated some Chipmunk flying hours in order to accomplish instrument flying practice. During the pre-flight brief my 'student' told me that he was Chipmunk qualified.

Once he was ensconsed in the rear cockpit, where practice instrument flying is usually conducted, we completed all the necessary checks and got airborne. General flying, airmanship and procedures were all performed to a good standard and the sortie progressed well.

After an accurate instrument recovery and overshoot in excellent weather conditions, my 'student' then asked if he could land the aircraft from the rear seat; I agreed. The circuit was accurately flown down to the latter stages of the final approach where a crosswind of five to ten knots was experienced. This was well within the aircraft limit and the capability of a typical UAS student pilot.

The initial round-out was somewhat high and, after descending a little further, my 'student' realised that the aircraft was drifting towards the edge of the runway. At this point, he sensibly called 'overshooting'.

Then, disaster struck. His overshoot action consisted of simply pulling the control column fully rearwards, entirely omitting any application of power whatsoever! With a high nose attitude, an idle power setting, and nothing on the clock apart from the maker's name, the aircraft surrendered and stalled. The starboard wing dropped viciously towards the grass.

Despite my scream of protest, and a full and rigorous application of power, left rudder and aileron (contrary to my CFS mentors), I was unable to prevent the lower (starboard) wing from striking the ground and slewing the aircraft through 45° to the runway centre line.

With power and controls applied, the aircraft became controllable and was immediately landed on the grass, pointing towards the control tower. Subsequent inspection revealed that the damage was slight - the starboard aileron was bent and there was a small dent in the wingtip.

It was only during completion of the subsequent 'Special Occurrence Report' that I discovered that my 'student' was a navigator with a PPL and had only flown a civilian Chipmunk before. As a consequence of that narrow escape, I thereafter made it a strict point to check the aircrew specialisation of anyone I ever flew with, even if their flying kit had a set of wings displayed. After all, the Army and Navy Stores are only too eager to sell surplus flying kit to any budding Walter Mitty.

DHC 1 Chipmunk T10

MAKING A MESS OF IT

It was a delightfully crisp winter's day in County Armagh. The unpolluted air was gin-clear (perhaps that should be poteen-clear) and I was enjoying myself. Northern Ireland Support Helicopter detachments were very enjoyable in 1971, particularly for a 22 year old bachelor who found that his tastes for black stout, Irish girls and Wessex flying were more than amply indulged. I was a fairly senior flying officer too, a second tourist (well, technically, even if the first tour was only a year in Sharjah) and fast approaching the magic figure of 1000 hours by clocking up 50 to 60 hours a month in Ireland. I was certainly the oldest and most senior member of the crew; the co-pilot was a pilot officer (remember when we had those on squadrons?) and the crewman a young sergeant air loadmaster. We were conducting an 'Eagle Op', deploying Marines rapidly and unexpectedly into fields adjacent to roads, in (usually unsuccessful) attempts to stop cars. This provided an ideal opportunity to demonstrate (ie 'show off') to the crew my easy mastery of anti-terrorist operations and my above-average flying and captaincy skills. Or so I thought.

The story really starts as we were returning to a forward operating base for lunch. The FOB was a collection of grim Victorian buildings in Armagh City and the headquarters for the Marines; they did a good lunch in the Mess too. The landing site was the barrack square, which was surrounded by the aforementioned grim buildings. It was a confined area for sure, but posed no problem at all for someone of my skill (not a lot) and experience (not a lot of that either). Wessex XR 517 and I were made for each other.

LC

My UHF safety call was quickly completed. We had three radios in all; the Captain normally used the UHF, the Co-pilot used the VHF/FM to talk to troops, and the Crewman the HF to talk to base. "Clear left, Martin?", I enquired. "OK. Gary, landing spot as before. Your directions", was the response. A man with my in-built natural authority could afford to use first names to his crew without sounding patronising. Then trouble struck: attention-getters, flashing lights and a strange feeling in the controls.

"Captain to Crew", (no time for informality now), "HYD 2 failure, disengaging the ASE (Auto Stabilisation Equipment: an early attempt at autopilot technology)". Oh joy - an 'easy' emergency, much favoured by QHIs and IREs, and therefore much practised. It was a golden opportunity to demonstrate to my crew my above-average flying and cap-taincy skills. Or so I thought.

"OK, I'll continue with the approach. Martin, tell the Ops Room we're unserviceable. Gary, tell Aldergrove we'll need a replacement cab". I then took a closer look at the flashing lights and gauges and suddenly realised that I would need the Crewman for the landing. "Belay my last; Martin: you take the HF and tell Base and ...er...."

"UP! UP! UP!" My rambling chatter was interrupted by a very urgent call from the Crewman. I grabbed a handful of collective (increased power sharply) and looked out (which I hadn't been doing) to get an extremely close view of a grim Victorian chimney. It was, in fact, much closer than I had ever seen a chimney before. A chastened and silent crew completed the landing to be greeted by an irate lieutenant colonel from the Marines whose rare moment of relaxation in the Mess had been well and truly spoilt when my approach had caused a cloud of soot to be blown out of the fire-place!

What were my problems? Complacency, overconfidence and appalling crew management certainly. However, the overriding fault was that by allowing myself to be distracted by a relatively minor emergency, I had gone 'head-in' at a critical stage of a confined area approach without even the benefit of the ASE. 'Fly the aircraft' is what the pilot should do. I didn't and very nearly flew into a building.

There are two final points. It was actually a HYD 1 failure (so I could have kept the ASE) but we never practised those; perhaps a lesson there for instructors/examiners on providing variety for their victims. Lunch that day consisted of nothing more than a NAAFI sandwich; for some reason, I wasn't welcome in the Mess.

Wessex HC2

LOCKED IN APPREHENSION

It was not a typical Malayan night. There was neither soft moonlight nor gentle breeze - nothing like that at all. It had been raining quite heavily all day but instead of clearing up in the evening, as it usually did, the cloud and rain persisted. Not heavy rain, but a continuous moderate fall from a sky that was totally obscured and very dark.

I was the Squadron QFI and it was my duty to familiarise all new Squadron pilots with flying conditions in Malaya. It was really quite a pleasant job since I felt that flying in Malaya was less hazardous, weather-wise, than in the UK. However, new pilots didn't know this and were always a little apprehensive at first, mainly as a result of dire predictions from people who really should have known better. The theatre training always included a period of night flying and it was due to take place for a newly arrived pilot that night.

The strip from which we operated in those days was rather short, surrounded by obstructions and totally unsuitable for night flying training. In fact, only one take-off and the final night landing was permitted to be undertaken there. Training circuits and landings were carried out at a much larger airfield a few miles away, after which we then returned to our own strip for the final touch-down.

I had a look at the weather, decided it was 'on' and arranged to start after dark. The aircraft was parked alongside the strip and, along with the new pilot, we started the pre-flight inspection. Having got about half-way round, I was called to the telephone to speak to the Controller at the main airfield, so I left the pilot to continue the inspection. On my return, he had finished and was boarding the aircraft. I went round to my side and got in beside him.

Because of the unsuitability of the strip and the inexperience of the new pilots, I always taxied the aircraft and did the first take-off myself, telling them to follow me through on the controls. I would then hand over control so that they could fly the few miles to the main airfield before beginning instruction proper. I started up and began taxying; I remember thinking at the time that the pilot was more than a little nervous as he was very tense on the rudder. However, this was not unusual in the circumstances and I refrained from comment as I felt it would only make him worse. In any case, it was necessary in the confined area to use the brakes to control direction most of the time anyway. We eventually lined up and completed the pre-take-off check satisfactorily, apart from the resistance from what I thought were two heavy feet on the rudder. At this point I ought to say that quite a lot of movement of the rudder bar is possible even if locked.

Having been cleared for take-off I applied full power against the brakes and away we went. Departure was not quite as usual because immediately the brakes were released and the aircraft moved forward, it swung sharply to starboard, despite the usual leading with port rudder.

A touch of brake brought the nose back pointing down the strip and we continued. However, the swing to starboard persisted and brake had to be used continuously in order to keep straight. All this time, I was quite convinced it was due to the other pilot being too heavy with his 'following through'.

I recall finally becoming airborne in a considerable swing which took me over the other aircraft parked on the dispersal and I distinctly saw some rather surprised ghostly faces looking up at me, obviously wondering what on earth the QFI was up to this time.

The speed, in the meantime, had increased to around 60 kts and I found that by application of bank it was possible to keep the aircraft straight. It was at about this moment, and not before time, that I had a horrible thought. We were away from the darkness of the ground and there, sure enough, when I turned to look, were the large red streamers flying in the slip-stream. The rudder lock was still firmly attached to the rudder.

What to do? I climbed up to 1500 ft or so and headed for the main airfield, thinking furiously. Having levelled off, I gingerly experimented and reduced speed until I could no longer keep straight by banking the aircraft. This occurred at a speed of around 55 to 60 kts. There was quite a side slip at this speed but it could be done. Since the fin was now at least twice its normal area, directional stability was much increased.

I confirmed the minimum control speed a couple of times and then flew around to line up on the main airfield's runway. I flew the approach at around 80 kts, slipping down towards the runway with the nose of the aircraft over to starboard. At the hold off I gradually reduced the power and, as the speed fell, increased the bank until I could no longer prevent the nose from yawing to port. As soon as the aircraft was lined up with the runway I levelled and put the wheels quickly and firmly on the ground in a rolling landing. And there it was, wheels on the ground and the use of the brakes to keep straight. I remember being very thankful that rolling landings were being taught on this aircraft at that time. We came to an uneventful halt, removed the offending lock and continued flying; but that first landing was the best I did that night.

WHAT A PERFORMANCE

GW

My introduction to Chipmunk flying could hardly by described as having gone 'according to the book'. There I was, an eager first tourist jet jockey on a Duxford day-fighter Meteor squadron, having flown but two types, namely the Harvard and Meteor. My revered Flight Commander, a former Chipmunk QFI with about 2000 hrs on type under his belt, finally acceded to my persistent pleading for a check-out in the Station Flight 'Chippie'.

We had a quick trip together, during which I remember being impressed by the small size of the loops that we flew and the close proximity of the ground when commencing a spin! So, duly checked out, I awaited the opportunity to go solo in my latest type. Reference to my logbook shows that more than 14 months went by before the great day came, although to tell the tale with absolute truth, I must say that, about a month after my 'dual check', I did scrounge 30 minutes in the back seat with another 'qualified' pilot.

On the day in question, I had just settled down to my first cup of coffee, having noted gloomily that I was not scheduled to fly until after lunch, when at least the long wait would be rewarded by a low-level 'Rat and Terrier' sortie. The Flight Commander stuck his head into the crewroom and asked: "Does anyone want to go up to Leconfield to pick up Bloggs?" It was a Friday, and Bloggs, the 'extra' flight lieutenant on the Squadron, was anxious to return to base for the weekend. In addition, on the way back, whoever did the trip was required to call in at Bovingdon and drop off the AOC's hat which had somehow been left on the Station on the previous day. Being the regular holder of the 'hog of the month' award, I got my bid in first, although I omitted to tell the new Flight Commander that my Chipmunk qualification was based on very limited experience. No bother. I scrounged a copy of the Pilot's Notes, got a friend to come out and show me how to start the thing and off I went.

During the 75 minute flight northwards, I twice carefully read the Notes and was beginning to feel quite 'seasoned' on type by the time I reached Leconfield. Bloggs was ready and waiting, but was somewhat surprised to see me, remarking "I didn't know you were qualified on the Chipmunk". I explained the situation as we got airborne and declared my intention of over-flying base and proceeding direct to Bovingdon to drop off the AOC's hat.

"But," said Bloggs, "you are going to have to refuel sometime and I think you ought to do that at base". He was no doubt conditioned by the thought of reaching home at the earliest possible time, but I have little doubt that he was also applying some of his QFI knowledge to our fuel consumption and fuel state! Eventually I was 'persuaded' to drop him off at base, but there was no way I was going to miss out on my 'Rat and Terrier' sortie through having to make an intermediate fuelling stop. I had done my fuel calculations most carefully and reckoned I would have at least a gallon or two in hand on my eventual return to base.

So, we landed on the grass light aircraft strip, where I disembarked my passenger. "Can't waste my precious fuel driving you all over the airfield can I?" Chuckling to myself, I took off again with a last look at Bloggs humping his parachute and other gear across the airfield!

Joining at Bovingdon along the approved entry corridor, I realised I was about to make my first Chipmunk landing on a smooth runway rather than on a bumpy grass strip. Being an experienced Chipmunk 'ace' by this time, I made a very respectable arrival. As I started to taxy towards the tower, I heard an American voice call for "Taxy clearance to the compass swinging area", (I was tuned to Bovingdon's Local frequency.) The Super Dakota involved was told to hold until the light aircraft had cleared, and I was instructed to "Expedite".

No sooner said than done! I gunned the throttle and started to scorch along the taxyway "just like Fangio". However, it suddenly dawned on me that the taxyway was turning to the left rather quicker than I could turn the aircraft at the speed I was travelling. Undaunted, I grabbed the hand-brake and pulled back on the control column, intending to check my rate of advance. To my intense surprise and alarm, I did the sharpest 'hand-brake turn' in the business. In fact, I swung through slightly more than 360° and finished pointing along the taxyway once more, but now travelling at a more or less sensible speed. Suffice to say, I was no longer a confident Chipmunk ace as I shamefacedly passed the AOC's hat to a waiting airman, and I will never forget that American voice saying "Bovingdon, I see the light aircraft has finished his performance. Am I now clear to taxy?"

By the way, about the only thing I did get right that day was my fuel calculation - and I see from the logbook that I managed to fit in my low level interceptions after all! Many flying hours later, I still feel most humble when I recall that particular day's antics. I suppose I must have learnt something from it!

LIGHTNING MOUTH MUSIC

I'm an ace, really. Your actual steely-eyed fighter pilot. Even passed my Individual Staff Studies Course. Bags of experience: multis, singles, groaners and wooshers. Forgotten more than most of my readers remember. More than 4000 hrs plus as a QFI, patter, patter, drone, drone and all that.

Took a lad flying in my BAe groundhog Lightning T5. Ignorant about flying - him, that is - so I shot him all the OK briefs. Pull this lever, don't pull that, feel like a sardine, disregard panic in left-hand seat; chute handle, starter buttons, getcher knee off the transmitter button, if your chute hasn't opened by 10,000 ft yell and I'll brief you on the way down, plus all the other professional patter.

Weather - icy. Cloud - 300 ft but I can see for miles; (about two). Terrain - snowy. Fuel restrictions up the ying-yang. OC Ops says wotchit. Strap in. Taxi out, muttering brake pressures and impress lad with fighter-type pre-take-off checks. Ready to go for reheat take-off. Brakes off, full cold power, pause, pause, select reheat. Sagging feeling like Jet Provost take-off and no accompanying and reassuring boom-boom. One reheat flickers. Finish take-off feverishly selecting and cancelling. Great. Finally get reheat in at 10,000 ft.

Erewego lad. You have control. Don't let 'er go supersonic in climb, as local mayor gets grumpy. At 30,000 ft cancel reheat: fly out to sea, watch fuel like hawk. In reheat for ten-ton tie. Dive through transonic; QFI mouth music. Hit Mach 1.6 and drag it all back saying priority, no paraffin. Lad is glider pilot so competent in Frightening. Looks at fuel. Thinx! Can demo superb low altitude acceleration if fuel and cloud OK. Leave wheels up. Break cloud. All looks fine. Plug in reheat. Hurtle from 200 kts to 600 kts in next to no time, all going well. Lad impressed. Me too. Below 300 ft, doing 600 kts, rack it round to go downwind for landing.

Woops. Viz too poor, airfield not in sight. Snow on ground, can't recognise normal features. Paraffin - minimum. Conclusion - lost and in trouble. Big trouble.

I got down, but not without recourse to all sorts of tricks. And later, when I thought about the events of that flight, I realised that young lads are impressed enough with flying any aeroplane without also having to be impressed by a Martin Baker parachute descent. More to the point, that sortie made me realise that despite my age and experience I had been behaving like a damn fool.

A GHOSTLY TALE

The task was to train Army pilots on Tiger Moths and Austers. We thought we worked reasonably hard and we also reckoned we gave value for money doing about three hours instructing on a normal flying day.

One quiet afternoon the Flight Commander came into the crewroom and announced: "I've got some news for you, men. We've all got to do practice instructing with each other. It's called instructor's continuation training and we've got to do two hours a month".

"Strewth!" was the incredulous reply. "Aren't we doing enough already? Is there anything else?"

The Flight Commander held up a soothing hand.

"Now hold your horses, men. I haven't finished yet. You'll be better off than ever with my idea. You're doing your whack already, I know. All we have to do is to get together in pairs, one does an hour solo while his mate sits on the ground, then you change over. At the end, you put both your names in the Authorisation Book and get two hours in your log for one in the air. With a bit of sharp pencil, we'll be quids in - but don't finish up with one man in two different aeroplanes at the same time! They won't wear that".

Thus was born the gentle art of ghosting.

DH82A Tiger Moth

Yours truly was flying mad at the time and did not mind any number of hours, so one fine Monday afternoon I climbed into a Tiger and flew happily off on one of the cross-country routes. I was not flying too high and, looking lazily around, I spied in a paddock on a large walled estate a big herd of the most unusual looking cows I had ever seen. As I turned and descended for a better look, they took fright and thundered off to the far end of the field. I followed them round and thus began a real rodeo, with me driving them from one end of the meadow to the other. They split up, came together again, made skidding turns at the fences with great clouds of dust coming from their hooves. I felt like Tom Mix with wings.

Eventually tiring of this sport, I flew home, signed the Book and went off to tea. As soon as I had left, Flying Officer 'N' went into the Flight Hut and saw that I had been solo. "Well, the miserable toad", he said to himself. "I haven't been doing anything. I'll put my name in with his and we'll both get the time". Which he did, poor sap.....

The following Thursday afternoon he came to me after being interviewed by the CFI. "Johnny", he asked, "what the hell did you do on Monday?" "Monday ?" I said innocently, "nothing".

"Well, somebody did something. I've just been on the mat because someone has complained direct to the Air Ministry that a pilot in a Tiger Moth beat up a valuable herd of bison on his estate. He got the serial number, and it was you all right. I'll have to tell the truth if there's going to be trouble, you know. I can't be a party to that kind of non-sense".

"That won't do", I pointed out quickly, "then you'll be in it for falsifying the authorisation and that'll be worse than ever. Anyway, you were with me, your name's in the book in your own writing. Not only that, you were captain because you're an officer and I'm only an NCO!" "You b.......!" he exclaimed. "Well, you'd better tell me exactly what we did".

I filled in the essential details for him and heard no more about it, apart from an interview with the Commanding Officer where my ghost was soundly ticked off for setting such a bad example to me!

A SPORTING PASS!

Active involvement in sport is one of the most important and enjoyable features of a military career, and long may it remain so. Nevertheless, aviators should be aware that sporting activity and aviation do not always mix well, as the following story illustrates.

Hawker Hunter

Some years ago, I was a student on a short but highly enjoyable tactical weapons course. Unfortunately, following a recent move of the Unit, a combination of a poor weather factor and variable serviceability led to much frustration. On bad weather days there were always rows of serviceable Hunters; when the sun shone, however, there were usually only two or three. On just such a day it was pretty obvious by lunch time that I wasn't going to get my next 1v1 sortie, as I was way down the pecking order, so I arranged, with the Squadron Ops officer's agreement, to have a game of squash that afternoon.

This activity itself was enough to turn any self-respecting SFSO's hair grey, for there was no proper squash court on the Station, merely a large, lidless, plywood box erected in the hangar which housed the SAR helicopters and sundry other bits of kit. There was a sort of net over the roof, but this offered little resistance to a ball travelling at any speed.

Anyway, my opponent and I had an excellent thrash round the 'court', interrupted only by the need for numerous expeditions into the hangar to retrieve the squash ball from places like the inside of a Whirlwind's cockpit or beneath a Siccard sweeper. Just as we were finishing, an airman came trotting over. "Excuse me, Sir, but you're wanted on the Squadron - could you speak to them at once". I duly established that 'they' had scraped together some more jets, and would I get down there soonest to do my sortie. I protested weakly, only to be forcibly reminded of the need to fly whenever serviceable jets and good weather coincided. I was also informed that if I didn't, my course wouldn't finish on time and I wouldn't get away for the weekend, etc, etc. I gave in!

Half an hour later I was climbing up into the training area in wide battle formation, trying desperately to slow down my pulse rate, stop sweating and work out how to avoid being shot down too often by the lantern-jawed, demi-god staff pilot in the other aircraft. We split for the first fight, turned in and passed canopy to canopy. I then promptly lost sight of my adversary, fumbled about into a left-hand turn and suddenly caught sight of him coming towards me in a level gentle right hand turn. He was almost exactly head on . . .

At that point, I simply could not think what to do. I just sat there, like a rabbit fixed in the headlights of a car, mesmerised, with this Hunter getting bigger and bigger in the windscreen, but quite unable to take positive action. After what seemed like an eternity, he suddenly flashed just over the top of my aircraft - so close that I distinctly heard the noise of his aircraft. To say I was terrified would be putting it mildly.

Luckily, fate intervened at that point in the proceedings when my trusty Hunter decided it had clearly had enough and suffered an obscure hydraulic snag which put one aileron only into manual. We broke off the exercise and went home carefully.

It transpired in the debrief that my opponent had also lost sight of me after our initial pass and, crediting me with far more skill than I possessed, was desperately searching his six o'clock for me when he heard the roar of my aircraft passing underneath! It must have been the closest encounter of any kind that either of us ever had.

There was no doubt that my ability to react quickly and correctly in a demanding situation had been severely degraded by the strenuous exercise I had undertaken immediately before flying. The moral is obvious. Play as much sport as you can, but never ever go flying until you have completely recovered from the after effects. Failure to do so could be as lethal as flying with a hangover.

INTIMIDATING SUPERVISION

Now we all know what CFS stands for, don't we? But what about cfs? Well, now you've had a ponder, mutter and mumble about it, I can reveal that for the purposes of this cautionary tale it relates to Cadet Flight Sergeant, which is an oddity found only in the ranks of the Air Training Corps. This particular little cfs has a salutary 'learned from that' story, one that even now causes him the occasional nightmare and memories of it can still bring a blush of shame to his cheeks.

The year is 19-something and the Chipmunk is still on its first set of mainspars. The aircraft is, however, well established in the Air Experience Flights (AEFs), whose groundcrews are already well versed in the art of sick bag removal. This particular cfs has been in the Corps for some time, holds A and B Gliding Wings and has loads of Chipmunk time to his credit. The upshot of all this is that he tends to think he has hacked the air sickness bit and reckons he would recognise the pre-flight briefing for cadets even if it were recited in Arabic - and, perhaps, especially if it were in Arabic. By and large, he is a diligent little chap who religiously empties his pockets of loose articles, wears soft soled shoes and generally tightens up his brain before entering any aircraft.

At the time of our story the RAF Station concerned was the abode of a particularly nasty piece of mobile invective in the shape of a SNCO who allegedly ate ATC Cadets for breakfast. His rationale for this was: (a) he used to be one; (b) they seemed to do more flying than him; (c) he hated working weekends; and (d) he was born with a malicious streak. It is therefore true to say that he frightened cadets rigid and even the boldest little cfs with several years ATC service trod lightly in his presence.

LC

On the day in question, perfect flying weather prevailed, aircraft remained serviceable, pilots turned up in bunches of a dozen and fought each other for front seats, and the local UAS had a brainstorm and loaned our AEF an aircraft. The upshot was that cadets bounced in and out of cockpits like yo-yos and the flying programme progressed with such speed that the little cfs cunningly decided to take the last slot of the day. Experience had taught him that this could be either the shortest or longest of the lot, depending on Met and aircraft availability; today, the latter possibility seemed more likely.

Alas, it was not to be. Come lunch time and our lad is about to march his flock off to the airmen's mess a mile or so distant when a squadron leader taps him on the shoulder. "I want an experienced body for the first sortie after lunch. Be strapped in at 13.30 sharp", he says, and nods towards a solitary Chipmunk lounging contentedly in the shade between two hangars. Cfs acknowledges, silently swears and moves the herd to the waterhole.

Needless to say, some bodies go missing during the lunch break and much range riding is needed before they can be marched back to the AEF crewroom. The result is that the pack arrives back near the hangars at 13.29, to be met by the SNCO who is doing a war dance and threatening murder if little cfs isn't strapped in double quick. Cfs therefore rapidly abandons his squad to another cadet NCO; he then notices that during lunch two more Chipmunks have arrived on the pan, while the original aircraft has moved, and the SNCO is rapidly disappearing into the hangar still surrounded by a cloud of invective.

Cfs tosses a mental coin with reference to the original parking spot, calls wrongly and is thereby half strapped in to the incorrect machine when the SNCO returns with a scathing comment about the lunatic stupidity of cadets, before inviting the little cfs to board the right aircraft.

Some rapid cockpit hopping ensues, before the cfs finally tumbles into the rear seat, only to find after sitting down that the left leg strap is trapped under the parachute. As the start checks are well advanced, he decides he's in deep enough mire already. He therefore makes do with what straps he has and stills his troubled mind with the thought that no one has had to bale out yet.

The Squadron Leader advises cfs that the reason for wanting an experienced body in the back is that the aircraft in question has just had a replacement compass fitted in the rear and it would be useful to know if it agrees with the one up front.

It is only at the holding point that the cfs register that his pockets are still full of junk. Again, he stills his conscience with the thought that it's only a compass tweaking jolly.

Twenty minutes later, the little cfs feels rather ill due to a stodgy lunch and his hunched position over a hot compass. Finally, the front office seems happy and announces in a loud voice, "As a reward, we'll now do some real aerobatics".

Ten minutes later, after a frantic session, the cfs is in the act of reaching for the little brown paper bag when he notices a gleam on the otherwise black cockpit floor. It's a sixpence and it shouldn't be there. A quick stab of the foot traps the offending coin firmly in place and its subsequent surreptitious removal when picking up the sick bag prevents the crimes of the cfs from becoming universally known. Nevertheless, he sure learned a hard lesson about flying, supervision and the effects of intimidation from that.

I'D STICK TO UCKERS IF I WERE YOU

You know what it's like when you've just finished training - Provosts, Vampires and Hastings (albeit as second pilot). A chap like that could easily handle a tame Chipmunk. It was kept on the Squadron as a perk for co-pilots bent on becoming inverted as a change from their normal *modus operandi*. I was no different. Two quick jousts in the back seat with an experienced (6 hrs) colleague up front; a 15-minute stall and circuit check-out with a QFI loaned by the RAF Museum, and off I went. Man, that was the life! Tear the skies up for 30 minutes, followed by a 4 hr debrief with my mates.

Next day, I went on route where pleasure of other sorts predominated and it was nearly a month before I was back at base. I was just going to sit on a navigator's donk (like a king in draughts) in a First Division uckers match when a voice shouted that there was a Chipmunk running outside and did I want it for an hour? Naturally, I did; I snatched up a 'chute, scribbled my mark in the Authorisation Book and bolted out to where the gleaming, throbbing machinery stood.

"That's odd. Was the cockpit like this last time? Still, they could hardly have changed it; everything looks too reesty (old) and here's the pole (control column), and the noise control (throttle) - so let's be off".

Taking off was no bother, I think, and I managed to find a nearby airfield where the powers that be were happy to let us budding aviators test our skills well away from the shiny Comets circulating at our own field. After I had located an unusually elusive channel change switch, I called the Tower and was cleared for landings and take-offs. Mind you, to be frank, by now I was beginning to have some misgivings. Maybe I should have asked for another check ride - still, steel the nerves old chap, you're nearly there.

My first landing was a ten-foot bounce from which I overshot; my second was worse! Impersonating a high altitude salmon is good fun, but as I lined up for the third stab I said to myself, "Lad, you had better keep it down this time, you can't spend the rest of your life airborne you know". The alternative, which flashed through my mind in glorious tech-nicolour, was too horrible to contemplate for long!

On this attempt I shot off the runway to the left, back across it and exited the other side before overshooting. It was then that a fatherly voice from the Tower said that if my intention was to destroy my aircraft, he would be grateful if I would do it on my own airfield. I set off home, the shame and the loneliness replacing the anxiety. Oh gloom!

My next problem was how could I keep on the deck back at base; but, as so often happens in life, my fears were groundless. The engine stopped as I crossed the threshold at about 20 feet. I was so petrified by this that I must have frozen in just the right pose, with the result that the Chipmunk landed herself. It was evidently something to do with some mixture lever gadget that has to be wiggled every now and again. At least I was down.

Now what? There was a Comet on finals and the Tower was shouting at me. The trouble was that I'd never started the beast before - I always made sure I got in when it was already running. Cue frantic search to find the right lever gadget. I espied a sign - 'To start pull knobbley'. I did - Bang! We rolled on down the runway.

"Expedite clearance up secondary runway", came a voice through the ether.

"It's blocked with a ridge of snow", said I. It was February and they had been sweeping.

"Another aircraft has just taxied that way", thundered the voice.

"Right", said I, promptly charging the wall of snow. The voice really ought to have said that the other aircraft was a Hastings. I rammed into the snow, stuck and the engine promptly stopped again. This time, in spite of frantic work on the wire starter thing, the engine did not pick up - fortunately perhaps, because I was not, at this stage in the proceedings, at all confident about taxying a Chipmunk backwards. The Comet overshot and a tractor appeared and towed me back to dispersal, where, with my hat pulled well down over my face, I tried to make the sanctuary of the crewroom without being spotted. However, as I skulked along in the shadows of a hangar, a large hairy arm latched on to my own and gently drew me into a small office. "Listen, laddie", said the owner of the arm, thrusting a pen into my hand, "If you ever fly any of these aircraft again, make sure you sign the Form 700 before getting airborne.... Sir!"

I suppose many readers will have a hard time believing that so much could happen during a 45-minute sortie, but let me assure you that it did, I am sorry to say. I'll leave it for you to see how many lessons could be learned. I still get adrenaline in my goose-pimples when I think about it. The only word of advice I would pass on is never interrupt an uckers match to fly in a Chipmunk!

FUELISH MISTAKE

DH82A Tiger Moth

The day had finally arrived when I was to fly my solo land-away cross-country in a Tiger Moth from Kidlington, Oxford, during my flying scholarship at the tender age of 17. My pilot log card, which I had taken hours to prepare, was secured to the top of my map with paper clips and I was ready to go. I set off for Portsmouth and enjoyed the unlimited visibility for a while. It was only when I could no longer see Smokey Joe, the chimney that was the visual homing beacon for Kidlington, that I got out my map and log card. Unfortunately, I carelessly raised them too far into the airstream, causing my log card to slip out of the paper clips - all my careful calculations fluttered gracefully down to earth while my heart fell with a more pronounced bump.

I don't think I panicked, but I recall having some strange thoughts. I could remember from childhood days in South Africa that large towns would sometimes have their names emblazoned in white stones on grassy hillsides and I wondered vaguely if Reading would be equally obliging. As quickly as I dismissed this idea, I pondered the possibility of dropping down and look at the odd signpost! Common sense ultimately prevailed and I continued south having decided that I should be able to sort out the coastline to find Portsmouth, which I duly did.

I joined the circuit and concentrated hard on the landing strip on this unfamiliar airfield. In fact, I concentrated so hard that I omitted to do all the good things one is supposed to do, like checking the final approach course before turning on to finals. Luckily, I did a great 'S' bend overshoot of the centre-line that allowed a Dakota to slide in ahead of me, whilst I overshot and left the circuit, praying that the pilot of the Dakota might forget about the lack of airmanship I displayed in turning across him on finals. Sometime later I returned to the circuit, rubber necking continuously, landed and taxied in, to park well away from the Dakota. Having paid my modest landing fee, I summoned a mechanic to spin the propeller for me. By now, my confidence was returning and I glared at the mechanic, who grabbed the propeller without doing my Kidlington-taught drills of chanting 'switches off, fuel on', etc. I smugly checked the magneto switches off and thought to myself how lucky he was that I was sufficiently careful to avoid the risk of causing the propeller to kick and possibly break his arm. Once I was started, I waved the idiot away and taxied towards the marshalling point. Fortunately, the engine stopped before I took-off, or else it would have been Portsmouth harbour for me, as I had failed to turn the fuel supply on when I was checking the magneto switches were off. The one mistake I didn't make that day was to try and salvage my pride by turning the propeller myself, or else I might have ended up chasing my Tiger Moth all round the Hippodrome. No, I ate humble pie in front of the noble mechanic who got me started again and off I went to Thruxton and back to Kidlington, uneventfully, I am happy to report.

I think I learnt a lot about flying from that. I have never considered myself to be a natural pilot and have a healthy respect for the unknown. I now recognise and acknowledge that I would not have been good fighter pilot material but I have had an uninterrupted and enjoyable flying career as a QFI and transport pilot, having become a stickler for check lists and standardisation. I now have an 'A' category and just under 7000 hrs but I still remember that trip from 20 years ago as if it were yesterday.

CG

SOMEHOW I SCRAPED HOME...

The months passed and such was the amazing rate of promotion that before the end of my first tour on Meteor FR9s I became a deputy-acting-unpaid-flight commander. Night flying was always a bit of a bore for us hairy low-level chaps because there was not very much to do except medium level cross-countries and circuits. On the night of the incident, though, we were deployed to a strange airfield while our own runway was being resurfaced, something that has happened once or more in each of my flying tours! We went through the usual briefing sequence and I tried to give an impression of alertness; after all, I was deputy-acting etc. As it happened, I did not feel too well and, luckily for my subsequent career, I mentioned this fact to another pilot. Then, I authorised a new pilot to do a sortie of approaches and circuits and I shot off into the velvety darkness. It certainly was a lovely night, with the stars twinkling above and the lights of the glittering cities below.

Some 40 minutes later, I was back in the circuit flogging away at two-engine approaches, single-engine approaches and the odd flapless landing to liven things up a bit. When I was downwind 'on one', I heard the young lad I had authorised also call downwind, but there was a marked absence of navigation lights. He was cleared to finals behind me and on we went. I called finals; he called finals. By this time, even the Tower was getting suspicious. So was I, and I overshot. The new pilot was told to overshoot and a few minutes discussion made it clear that he had been doing his circuit at another airfield some 20 miles away, which was certainly well lit up since that runway was being resurfaced too and large construction machines were moving up and down it.

However, the bitter bit was still to come. I turned downwind again, meanwhile fuming over the idiocy of junior pilots, turned finals, called three greens, held the speed exactly right and had my efforts rewarded by the grinding noise of two engine nacelles making expensive contact with the concrete. (One thing to be said for the Meteor was how well it landed without wheels).

The Board of Inquiry was actually very good about it all. The fact that I had said I was not feeling well was confirmed by the other pilot and the doctor who examined me after the accident found that my blood pressure was up. A kindly engineer discovered some marks inside an undercarriage door that gave a million-to-one possibility that the wheels had been down and had then mysteriously collapsed. So, I got away with a few tense minutes with my Station Commander (who was a very fierce officer indeed) and two weeks' sick leave.

Morals:
- ✈ Do not fly if you do not feel fit - even as deputy-acting etc.
- ✈ Never allow yourself to be distracted from the job in hand when in the air.
- ✈ Don't take it for granted that your Board of Inquiry will be as considerate as mine.
- ✈ If you are a young lad (or an old one), always make sure you are landing at the right airfield!

EMOTIONAL TRIGGER

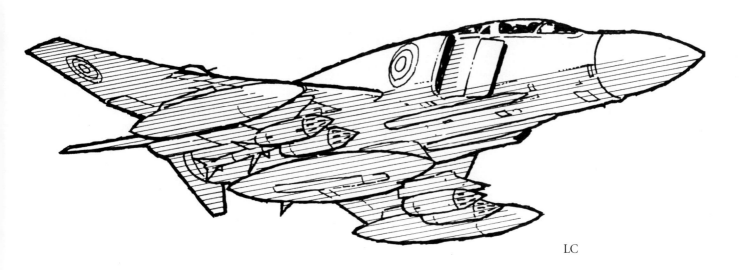

LC

When the Quick Reaction Alert (QRA) duty is handed over from one squadron to another, careful co-ordination is required to ensure that both sets of squadron operations, as well as the crews, the controlling authority and the Master Radar Station, all know exactly which aircraft and crews are on what state of alert at any particular moment. A scramble in the middle of a handover has been known to be very embarrassing.

On the station where I was serving, we found a good way of reducing the cock-up potential was for the squadron that was taking over 'Q' to arm and declare on state its two aircraft. The squadron that was standing down would then either tow its two aircraft out of the 'Q shed' or fly a practice two-aircraft scramble and download the weapons after the sortie.

On one particular changeover, as our Squadron was standing down, we decided to man the 'Q' aircraft with two fresh crews and fly supersonic missile attacks for the benefit of one of our navigators, who was working towards operational status. Naturally, one has to be very careful when flying fully armed aircraft. There are, therefore, precise orders concerning weapon switch selections, plus additional restrictions on pointing one's aircraft and its infra-red missiles at another while in flight. Furthermore, although it was to be a training flight, it was obviously advisable to select two operational pilots to fly the aircraft. I was the QWI for my Squadron and, as I was to lead the sortie, I selected another pilot with considerable experience.

The inexperienced navigator and I were to fly together. We briefed to fly the first two attacks with an option on a third if there were any problems. Two good attacks were required for a 'DCO' (duty carried out).

The navigator was useless - really useless. The first two attacks were complete failures because he couldn't sort out the fairly simple intercept geometry involved. What is more, he couldn't even remember the simple pre-attack arming and radar checks. In those days, it was customary for the navigator to call out the pilot's armament switch selections and his own radar switch selections before the start of each attack.

I exercised my briefed option. By the start of the third attack, I was upset by the navigator's incompetence and frustrated that he seemed to be coping so badly after my 'excellent' briefing. It is hard to explain how I felt. Somehow, I wanted to generate a little urgency and enthusiasm for he gave the impression of being bored and uninterested. I also wished to impress upon him that the attack could be flown as briefed.

So, I decided to 'talk' him through. I called out the checks as we turned on to the attack heading and, after radar lock on, manoeuvred the aircraft for a head-on Sparrow missile shot. Thinks: "Why can't this dummy do it like me? Here we are, perfect geometry, coming into range". I made the appropriate radio call to signify that the head-on attack was complete, pulled the trigger twice to simulate firing the radar-guided missiles and banked and pulled to start the re-attack for the a missile shot. As I did so, I glanced momentarily at the missile status panel to confirm that two of the lights had gone out, which would confirm the simulated launch and success of the attack. There were no lights at all. "What the ... Ohmigawd . . ."

With a fully-armed aircraft, I had run through a complete attack sequence and in the middle of the firing envelope, head-on with a radar lock, I had pulled the trigger twice. The missiles didn't go because when I had called out the pre-attack checks I didn't actually make the selections. What really made me feel sick then (and still does now) is the knowl-edge that I had gone into 'auto' and was reacting as trained: I still cannot understand how I failed to make the selection in accordance with the drill.

As the QWI and 'weapons expert' on the Squadron, as a supervisor, and as someone who was considered reliable and whose advice was usually deemed sound, it took me some time to regain my inner confidence and self-esteem. However, I learnt two valuable lessons. First, never ever allow yourself to get upset or angry in the air. The emotion of the 'just wait till I get on the ground, I'll get the *****' leaves little or no brain power for anything else. Second, in peace, the understandable desire to improve operational capability must not become so overwhelming that we lose sight of the aim. In retrospect, I believe that on fast jet squadrons most of us are hooked on operational capability and that we don't really give much thought to safety. There has to be a balance.

F-4 Phantom

FLIGHT SAFETY IS EVERYBODY'S JOB

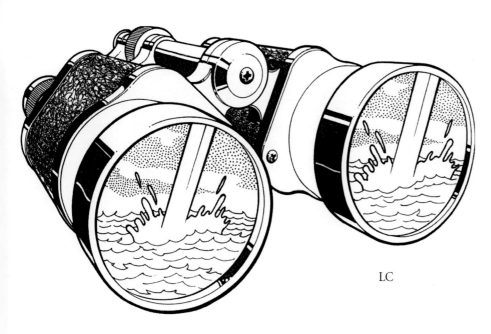

LC

It was a cold Spring morning when I arrived at the Tower for work. As Duty Runway Controller I was required to report for duty 15 minutes after the Tower opened, in accordance with local orders. It was three months since my 'cat' and I was full of the joys of spring. After all, this was my second tour as a runway controller, so I knew it all - at least I thought I did.

I collected the keys, rations and paperwork from the Admin Office and set off for another day's graft. While carrying out the daily inspection of the caravan, I found an earthing lead with a missing clamp. It turned up lying on the floor of the vehicle and a quick check with the GRF revealed it had not been reported the previous evening at cease flying. "Can you fix it now?" I asked the bleary eyed fitter.

"Sorry mate, I'm night watch and just going off duty," came the reply.

"Look, I can't switch on the mains without a proper earth. It'll only take you half a minute, can't you do it before you go off?" I asked him again.

"No, the day watch will be here soon. Anyway, it's not our job; earth leads are GEF problem," I was told.

That left me no choice but to set up on the end of the runway, call out the duty fitter and inform the Tower that the caravan was unserviceable. Lack of mains power meant that I had no radio and no heating, but I still had the telephones and Hadley (intercom box), which were on a separate circuit.

The fitters arrived just as the first aircraft of the day started engines. Frustration was beginning to set in now, as I was not following my normal routine.

"How long before it's fixed?" I asked.

"A while yet," the fitter said, "because the other clamp is only hanging on by a few strands, so that needs mending as well".

"The first pair are beginning to taxy, can't you do a quick repair, until they're airborne?" I asked, biting my nails.

The aircraft were just approaching the holding point when I was at last given power to the equipment. Quickly, I switched on the ARC 52 radio in time to hear the pair call for 'take-off'. Turning round, I looked towards the runway, but could not see it because of the heavy condensation on the windows. After furiously wiping them clear, I picked up the binoculars and, in the short time left, started to check both aircraft. I checked the right hand aircraft - no problems there. Then I saw the left hand aircraft was venting slightly from the starboard wing. It stopped as the engines ran up to full power, which was normal, but I decided to keep an eye on it since a recurrence would mean it was unserviceable.

Both aircraft then released their brakes and began the take-off. The left-hand aircraft's reheat was slow to light on the number two engine and this further engaged my attention, but apart from that the take-off was normal. When they had disappeared, I realised that I had not re-checked the right-hand aircraft on the take-off run.

Seven minutes later, one of the pair crashed into the North Sea. For three weeks, I waited to know the cause, all the time haunted by the thought that it might have been a hydraulic failure to the aircraft I had not re-checked, and that maybe I could have spotted it. Subsequently, the Board of Inquiry discounted hydraulic failure, instead attributing the cause to a fouling of the control runs by an unknown object.

The episode taught me several lessons. I now arrive at work in plenty of time to check all the equipment thoroughly and I am particularly conscious to ensure that all the aircraft in a section receive thorough and timely attention. When faced with the 'not me, I'm airframes' routine, I explain my story, since it's my belief that everybody's job is somehow ultimately connected with aircraft safety.

I would hate anybody else to have to endure those same worrying three weeks.

BOMBS AWAY - NOT!

The outbound leg across the English Channel had been uneventful and my heart was full of pride. They had let me lead the Squadron for a dive bombing attack on a radar station and now we were over Normandy turning at 8000 ft. With confident terseness, I gave my instructions - "Carefree, echelon starboard, go. Camera switches on. Bomb switches on. Leader going down to port in 15 seconds".

The target stood out just ahead of the port wing tip. The Channel glinted brightly in the sunlight beyond and the '88 mills' (anti-aircraft artillery) had apparently not yet suspected what we were intending.

I peeled off to port, pushed the nose down for the customary steep dive, watched the speed build towards 500 and centred the ring-sight on the radar tower. I fired and the thump-thump of the four guns was a reassuring proof of my invincibility. Closer now and the target was large and steady in the sight. Left thumb on the bomb release, hold a moment, press now and start to pull, but remain parallel with the ground while streaking for the water line and relative safety.

As I climbed over the sea and looked around for the others to catch up and reform, my number two called. "Red one, you've got two hang-ups"...

A house of cards couldn't have collapsed quicker than my elation but, in extremis, the mind and reflexes work quite involuntarily. Of their own volition, my eyes focused on the selectors. As any idiot knows, the dropping switches must be on as well as the arming switches if the bombs are to be successfully released. Mine, however, were not.

An extraneous Power analysed the situation and took control. My right hand reached out and flicked the switches down, the hand came back onto the stick and rocked it sharply side-to-side whilst simultaneously my left thumb

LC

pressed the release. The sequence lasted about an hour in my mind but only a second in time, for my number two was already calling that the hang-ups had gone!

Pride was saved. At the debrief, there was a murmur of sympathy, instead of the acid of contempt. I learned a lesson, but my conscience paid the price. However, it was well worth it. We were still a team and they would happily follow me again. But little did they know ... Even in war one can learn about complacency and flying.

A TWITCH IN TIME

Hawker Hunter FR10

I was flying Fighter / Recce Hunters in the Middle East at the time and since we only had four aircraft, the pilots enjoyed one of those rare opportunities always to fly their own aircraft. As a result, it was pretty easy to identify each aircraft's particular quirks and unique foibles.

One of those four aircraft managed to develop a rather intriguing peculiarity all of its own, for it became quite 'twitchy' in pitch. As a result, it had a tendency to 'tuck in' when pulled into a turn and it regularly exceeded 7g on the range. However, this was always easy to do in the Mk 10 and did not excite any special interest. It was not until the Squadron returned from armament practice camp and fitted 100 gallon and 230 gallon tanks for our normal recce work that the problems became even more marked.

I took the aircraft on the second sortie following tank refitting. It had been snagged on the first sortie for 'twitchiness' and some investigations had been carried out. But aircraft 'twitchiness' is difficult to describe and even more difficult to pin down. As a result, no fault was found and even though this characteristic was most noticeable just after take-off, there was no suggestion that the aircraft was uncontrollable. In fact, as is so often the case on these occasions, I found myself asking if I was not imagining the situation or perhaps exaggerating the effects of a slightly over-sensitive elevator. Anyway, I pressed on with the flight, which was to be a high-low-high sortie, with the first target just after the descent to low level - at a time when the aircraft would still be heavy with fuel.

In order to obtain a decent photograph of a small target, it was advisable to slow down, drop some flap, and get low and close in order to reduce blur. I did, cruising by the objective at about 200 kts and 100 ft or so, which was neither illegal nor ill-advised. Having flown by the target, I then turned quite hard through 90º onto the next heading, which also gave me the chance to take a quick look over the shoulder at the receding target.

The aircraft flicked - viciously. Rapidly, I found myself in the traditional 'line-shoot' situation: "There I was, upside down at 100 ft with nothing on the clock, etc". I was able to recover control, but only just, and the sands of Arabia came very close to receiving me. Needless to say, I had frightened myself so thoroughly that I headed straight back to base.

The investigation took quite a while. Several times, it was tempting to flight test the aircraft again to try to get more 'gen', but common-sense prevailed. They found the problem eventually. The aircraft had a fault of some sort associated with the rear internal fuel tanks. But that wasn't the end of it....

It had been decided that, until spares became available, the rear tanks should be blanked off and the aircraft was 'red-lined' to that effect. Unfortunately, those responsible had blanked off the rear tanks **whilst they were still full of fuel** - and, since these tanks always fed first, the aircraft had a permanent centre of gravity problem!

The lessons to be learnt from this story may be reasonably easy to pick out, but the thing that I can never forget is this: if the Hunter had crashed, no one would ever have known what caused the accident. There certainly wouldn't have been any fuel left in those rear tanks, would there?

ABOVE UNCHARTED TERRITORY

LC

Some years ago as a junior pilot (JP) on my first squadron in Singapore, we were detached to Hong Kong to restart helicopter support for the Army in the colony. As a young pilot I was given the easier tasks to do, and finding my way around the colony wasn't too difficult (those who have been there will know what I mean - there are plenty of landmarks).

About two weeks into the detachment, the tasking was easing off, so the Flight Commander decided that some of us needed extra navigation training, which was to be combined with underslung load training. The idea was that the first aircraft would take a load out to an island, drop it and pass the grid reference back to the second aircraft, which would take off five minutes after number one. Number two would collect the load and drop it elsewhere, before passing the next grid reference to me as number three. I, in turn, would continue the system.

My first lift went all right and I continued doing some authorised low flying while waiting for the next pick-up. My crewman had the maps and charts down the back - I had retained only the 1/4 million scale as I didn't need further maps and he needed the navigation training. Well, I thought he did anyway. Suddenly, the intercom went quiet and then the crewman announced "Oops - your maps have just blown out of the door". "Very funny", said I, but he was right. I did a 180º turn and there were my maps floating gently to earth like leaves from a tree.

"Right", said I, full of captaincy, "you lost them - you go and get them". With that, I landed on a flat piece of ground nearby and despatched the crewman to collect them.

About five minutes later, I heard my call sign on the radio. It was the pilot of the second aircraft trying to pass me the next grid reference. I copied it down and acknowledged the call. But where was my crewman? I couldn't see him, so I lifted off to try and attract his attention. Didn't want to be caught napping, did I?

Where on earth was he? I couldn't see him anywhere. The young on-the-ball JP was becoming a little worried by this stage. Perhaps the crewman had fallen and hurt himself! There was that voice on the radio again, this time wanting to know if I had dropped the load yet. "No, not yet," was my reply. Panic stations now. Couldn't admit to losing my maps, could I? Where was he? There was that voice again. Thinks - I'd better tell them what has happened so they can continue without me. So I said, "Lost my maps - crewman recovering them for me". Voice by now a little angry says "Where is your crewman?" Of all the questions I didn't want, that was the one. I was then forced to admit that I had lost my crewman as well.

Frantic now! Where the heck was he? At last I found him sitting under a bush folding a map. Great, I thought, he's found them. When he climbed back on board, everything turned completely to worms for the only map he'd been able to find was one for the other side of the colony, which was of no use at all.

The young on-the-ball JP was then forced to admit on the radio that he had to return to base short of maps. Needless to say, when the others came back later I got 'absolute stick'.

What did I learn from that? I realised I didn't know the colony as well as I thought - familiarity had bred contempt. I learnt that both members of a crew should have maps for the job in hand. Also, I learnt a couple of embarrassing lessons from that smiling, experienced crewman; though I still don't know to this day whether or not the maps were lost accidentally.

A PAIN IN THE NECK

Gnat T1

Some years ago, I was employed as a composite tradesman on the handling flight of a well known advanced jet training station.

This particular day was not very nice to begin with and, as it wore on, it got worse. Gusting winds, heavy rain showers and intermittent low cloud were frequent, which meant that most of the flying was being done away from the home base area. However, there were good diversion fields and aircraft were recovering singly to base.

In the early afternoon came the news that one formation of three Gnat trainers had diverted to Ballykelly and planned to 'recover' sometime later in the afternoon. Then came the bad news! The only Palouste air starter trolley at Ballykelly was unserviceable, so could we arrange to recover the aircraft?

As it happened, the Gnat could be started by two methods. First and foremost, there was the Palouste. Secondly, it was possible to use four air bottles with a very antiquated pressure control system attached to them. The latter unit could be strapped into the rear seat of a Gnat if the dinghy pack was removed, but this was a fairly difficult job if you wished to avoid fouling the rear control column.

As someone with a fair degree of flying experience in the Gnat, I was asked if I could go to Ballykelly and 'rescue' the three aircraft. Pinch nose, blow hard, ears pop, "Yes", I replied. Two hours later I was airborne in a Gnat with the antiquated air starter strapped securely in the rear seat of another Gnat.

We arrived at Ballykelly and I fitted the air starter boxes to the air bottle trolley - we had brought two, just in case. There were five aircraft to start; three to be rescued plus two rescuers. Each aircraft would require up to 400 lb of air per start. From a full set of air bottles, I could expect no more than five starts and the last would be fairly slow with a very high jet pipe temperature. However, the blow-off disc on the air starter indicated 3600 lb pressure, so I crossed my fingers and hoped for the best.

All five started, although the last was a bit reluctant. Incidentally, I must say here that pulling a heavy set of air bottles round while wearing an immersion suit is not to be recommended as good sport.

I then dismantled the two air starter boxes and strapped them into the rear seat of the fourth Gnat. I ran across to the fifth Gnat, clambered into the rear seat and started strapping in. The pilot taxying said, "Harness tight and locked?" "Yes", I said. "No", I thought, for the anti-g strap was still undone. I turned the quick release button and banged it, but nothing happened. I hit it again and the straps fell out. I hastily started re-strapping in. The aircraft was rolling, so I took my feet off the rudder pedals and foot brakes while I did so.

Just as we got airborne the harness locked into position and I sat back and relaxed, watching the scenery as the aircraft flitted across the sea at 50 ft to keep under the mist. All too soon, with a quick run and break - $5^1/2$g - we landed back at Valley.

At this point, it should be explained that, unlike the Martin Baker seat, the Folland Gnat ejection seat does not have pins, simply a lever which moves horizontally through 90° to starboard. So, to all Gnat pilots or ex-Gnat pilots, reach out for your ejection seat safety handle. Awkward, isn't it? But it's a lot more awkward if it's still sticking in the back of your neck - like mine was!

That's right. I'd flown all the way across the Irish Sea at low level with a safe seat. Oh, I definitely learnt about flying from that!

Gnat T1

COULDN'T SEE THE WOOD FOR THE TREES

As my career draws fairly uneventfully towards its close, I find myself in one of the RAF's remotest posts - you won't guess where, so don't try! However, despite this isolation, I still see Air Clues and other pithy writings from the Flight Safety world and it occurred to me that an incident in my early flying life is distressingly apposite, even now.

Picture the young me, fresh and enthusiastic from the flying training machine and on my first squadron tour with a Meteor FR9 squadron in Germany. For the tactical recce role, we were then allowed down to 50 ft almost anywhere: what hilarious fun we had frightening chickens, knocking over sailing boats with jet-wash and roaring over the Mohne Dam. My rude awakening - discounting a low-level cross-country when I didn't bother to map-read because I knew the route so well and then found myself some 20 miles from the border on the wrong side - came on an early morning low-level photo sortie over relatively unknown terrain. A quick self-briefing, draw some lines on the map, mark off the minutes, sign the Form 700, light the fires and away I went. If not into the wide blue yonder, at least into the murky, yellowy gas which passed for the lower atmosphere in Western Europe.

Once I was well settled into the first leg and over open countryside, I got the Meteor down as low as I dared at a steady 360 kts. After about 20 minutes, I had the strangest feeling that I was not really quite as certain of my position as any good pilot-navigator should be. I ought to explain at this point that the grubby map (why have I always been stationed within half-an-inch of the join between two sheets?) was usually held in the left hand or dumped on the cockpit coaming during quiet spells. Anyway, after a quick check ahead to make sure that there were no pylons or children's kites in the way, I stuck my head in the cockpit, unfolded the map a trifle and in a second or two verified where I was. On looking up, I was far from elated to find that I was flying down a firebreak in a large wood, with pine trees well above me on both sides. Worse still, I was still descending! What felt like a 10g pull-up was succeeded by several minutes during which the adrenaline coursed freely through my body.

All right, nothing much actually happened; there was no adroit fighting with the controls - just a ham-fisted reaction and I lived. But there is a moral and a pretty important one, which is: if you have to work inside the cockpit, make sure that you have enough height to do so safely. Looking back I can see that this incident isn't novel or extraordinary for similar things are still happening at regular intervals. In fact, that is the thing that disturbs me now.

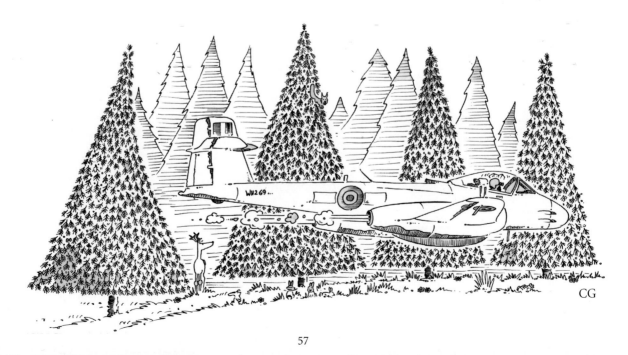

CG

ON A WING AND A PRAYER

Percival Procter

One Monday morning when I was almost at the end of my JP wings course, the Flight Commander announced that a volunteer with piston experience was required to fly an aircraft to Oxford. Like all the other students on the course, I had a fair amount of Chipmunk time from my days with the UAS, and I was one of a large number of volunteers. After eliminating those without PPLs, three of us remained and we obtained details of what proved to be an interesting experience. The task was to fly a Proctor from Woolsington to Kidlington, where it was to be delivered to its owner.

Naturally, none of us had ever flown a Proctor, but we soon discovered that one of these aircraft was stored at RAF Ouston, which was our relief landing ground. This Proctor was carefully examined and, as there were no Pilot's Notes available, we borrowed a set of Piston Provost Notes from one of the instructors. By nonchalant questioning we learnt something about supercharged engines and variable pitch propellers. All appeared quite straightforward and on the Wednesday afternoon I went to Woolsington to take a look at the aircraft to be flown south. I discovered it had single controls, the second set having been removed to reduce weight when it had been used for racing. I also made a short attempt at taxying, which proved difficult as only one brake worked properly. The Certificate of Airworthiness Notes which I was able to obtain listed a stalling speed but little else. When advised that the aircraft had only single controls, one volunteer immediately opted to visit his girlfriend at the opposite end of the country and it required severe arm twisting to persuade the other volunteer to come along. He became my navigator.

Saturday morning loomed wet and windy with an extremely low cloud base, but the two of us set off for Woolsington, collecting my girlfriend on the way. We checked in with the Met Office and were advised that a clearance was expected mid-morning, so we elected to wait and see. We listened with interest to each report from departing aircraft and were on the point of leaving ourselves when a very well-equipped Piper radioed that he was returning due to bad weather, so we decided to delay again.

Eventually, we considered the weather to be satisfactory and made ready to go. After some struggle, we got the Proctor going and proceeded to take off with some fairly wild swings and vast over-revving of the engine. With my navigator shouting "watch the airspeed", we clawed our way into the sky and I realised that girlfriend plus spare wheels and week-end baggage had created a considerably aft centre of gravity. However, after some mildly anxious moments, order was restored and we proceeded to follow the A1 south; so much for navigation! It was fortunate that many of the RAF stations down the A1 were closed for the weekend because the aircraft was fitted with a very poor four-channel VHF radio, with only two of the channels working. Fortunately, one of the frequencies was that of Kidlington. After a fairly pleasant and uneventful flight, we called up Kidlington and were advised that they were expecting us.

We were some distance from Kidlington when there was a 'combine call' that the wind was above solo limits and that solo students were to divert. As can be imagined, this news caused some consternation, for I was quite sure that my limits were very low and that the wind was certainly above them. We carried out a standard join into the circuit and made a very careful approach, but there was no way we were going to land with a 25 kt crosswind so I overshot and, in what I hoped was a confident voice, asked if it would be possible to land into wind (Kidlington was then all grass). This appeared to surprise the Tower, who clearly hadn't thought of this simple solution to the crosswind problem, in addition to giving a much shorter landing run. As we were the only aircraft airborne, permission was granted and, this time round, all went well. In fact, it went so well that I even surprised myself with the quality of the landing.

We were met by the owner, who, it transpired, had never flown, was nearly 60 and hadn't realised that the aircraft had single controls. He commented that he had heard Proctors had a tendency to flick in the turn if the speed was too low! He also produced the log books for me to sign and I duly discovered that his aircraft hadn't flown for over a year - and then for only 20 minutes. I discovered later that the aircraft failed its Certificate of Airworthiness due to deterioration of the glue in the wooden spars. I learned from that flight!

SHIPS (NOT) PASSING IN THE NIGHT

Who was Andrea Doria and what did she have to do with Flight Safety? Those with long memories will recall that she was an ocean liner that in 1956 collided at night and in poor weather in the North Atlantic with the liner Stockholm. Both ships apparently had radar contact with the other for some 30 minutes before the collision. Realising that they were on a collision course, each altered heading. Unfortunately, they turned in opposite directions, which yet again put them on a collision course. Realising this, both vessels reversed their turns. This jousting continued until the ships collided, whereupon the Andrea Doria sank.

Flying a red and white pursuit ship on a dual low-level navigation exercise over East Yorkshire, I saw a Jaguar in front of me, about 4 miles away, on a collision course. Good early spot, thought I; I had plenty of time to call the tally to my student, but as it was an early navex for him I didn't want to deviate from track or time unless I absolutely had to. I took control and watched the Jaguar carefully for a few seconds to see if he took any avoiding action. I also descended to 250 ft, which I judged would give adequate height separation from the skylined Jaguar. The Jaguar, to my surprise, also appeared to descend. Realising that we were closing rapidly, I then turned right and climbed, intending to keep him in sight and pass behind him. He must have seen us just before I started my manoeuvre, for I was then aware that he had turned left and was also climbing. I tightened my turn, lost sight of the Jaguar altogether, held my breath for a few split seconds and then, with my heart pounding madly, recovered the aircraft to track and speed as the Jaguar was seen clearing the area.

What did I learn from that? First, that keeping on track and time has absolutely zero priority when compared to avoiding a mid-air collision. Secondly, if you spot an impending confliction, don't play 'chicken'; take action early to remove the conflict. Thirdly, I learnt how quickly an early spot can turn into a real frightener. It was over for me in a few seconds and we didn't quite collide. But what a harrowing 30 minutes it must have been for the watch officers on board the Andrea Doria and the Stockholm!

Sepecat Jaguar

PRIDE GOES BEFORE A FALL

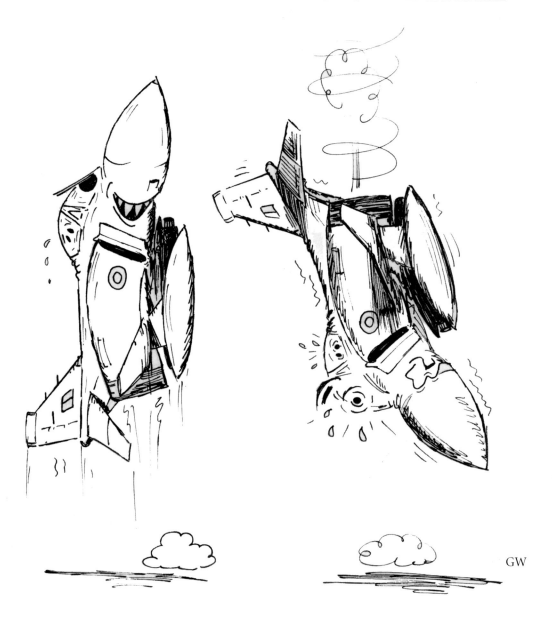

GW

"The Phantom is known to have a tendency to depart from controlled flight when the controls are mishandled at high angles of attack, particularly if aileron is used." How many times had I briefed that?

I had accumulated more than 1500 hrs in the Phantom and also had a good share of air combat experience. In the course of my training and squadron flying, I had frequently exceeded the normal maximum AOA and had occasionally seen the needle of the AOA gauge on the 'stops'. This was unintentional, as the aircraft does not turn too well in that condition. However, it was still controllable, as long as aileron was not used. Extremely low airspeed was no problem either, as long as one kept within the AOA limits - and the tailplane was effective in this respect even at speeds which the airspeed indicator did not register. I was therefore confident in my own and the aircraft's performance if I happened to get outside the normal limits. However, since the aircraft doesn't turn well at high AOA, I did my best to avoid those situations if at all possible.

One day, four aircraft were detached from our wing to participate in a Maxeval Exercise at Bitburg, which was home for the European F-15s of the United States Air Force. Our task was to fly three sorties a day, without RAF ground support, in two Phantom versus two F-15 air combat missions. Our aircraft were fitted with two underwing fuel tanks, carried a gun pod on the centreline and also had an inert Sidewinder missile for acquisition. Needless to say, this gave the F-15s a certain advantage.

The first few days resulted in our being soundly beaten by the F-15s and I was becoming ever more determined to do better.

During one engagement, when we had gone from a radar environment into the visual, I found myself separated from my wingman as I was attacking one of the pair of F-15s. He was higher than me and I went into a nose high head-on pass with the F-15 going down my port side. He went into a very rapid left hand turn across my tail. I had my nose high and turned, slowly to the right, while cancelling reheat in the hope that I could get the F-15 to fly out ahead of me. He finished up on my right-hand side about 500 yds away on a parallel flight path and slightly ahead, at about my speed. At this stage, my speed was decaying rapidly, as indicated by the flying controls becoming less effective, but I wasn't about to look into the cockpit and miss a move by the F-15. My navigator meanwhile was concentrating on keeping visual contact with my wingman and the other F-15.

As the speed reduced, the F-15 turned towards me hoping, I assume, to position for a guns kill. Due to my decaying airspeed, and the fact that he was slightly ahead, it very quickly became obvious that instead of falling in behind me, he was going to hit me. Up to that stage, I had been flying at zero g, and the noses of both our aircraft had fallen slowly until they were at 30° above the horizon. To try and avoid a collision, I attempted to get my aircraft above his, but as soon as I moved the stick back I was in heavy buffet and my flight path did not change. Just as he seemed about to hit me, I pulled the stick right back to the stops, which must have given me a few degrees of AOA. At that moment the F-15 overbanked and passed just under my fuselage, going nose low. I immediately pushed the stick fully forward and then applied full left aileron to follow him on his descent, for I was still 'fighting' and thought I could get into position for a Sidewinder heat-seeking missile shot.

My aircraft instantly rolled right and the nose sliced to the right. At that stage my altitude was about 18,000 ft and the height of the ground was about 3000 ft AMSL. I instantly centralised the controls and held the stick, fully forward. A glance at the AOA gauge showed it coming off the stops and starting to read a sensible figure, while the airspeed indicator read about 80 kts. I felt my weight lighten in the seat. I was happy we weren't going to spin! My aircraft continued to roll to the right and the nose dropped to what appeared to be the vertical and then oscillated about 10° either side. The speed started to increase slowly and I was able to control the AOA. I informed my navigator that I had regained control.

The roll stopped after about two revolutions and, as the speed increased to 180 kts, I selected 19 units of AOA (max lift) in order to recover from the dive. The height was about 12,000 ft and I unfortunately entered one of the puffy white cumulus clouds that dotted our exercise area. Maintaining a constant AOA, I recovered the aircraft wings level at about 7000 ft and eventually popped out of the side of the cloud 4000 ft above the ground.

During the 'hundreds' of air combat briefings I must have given over the years, I have always stressed that if you find yourself outside airspeed or AOA limits you must cease fighting immediately and recover to safe flight before manoeuvring further. In this case, the cause of the departure from controlled flight, apart from my pride and the will to win, was the sluggish tailplane response at low airspeed. Even though I had the stick fully forward, the AOA had not reduced sufficiently when I applied full aileron. The bottom line - I should have practised what I preached.

One other observation worth making is that I soon learnt the Phantom really does lose as much height as they say when recovering from loss of control.

DUCKING AND DIVING

The Tides Reach Hotel at South Sands, Salcombe, Devon features a fresh water pond some 40 yds from the high tide mark. The pond is constantly refreshed by a small stream and is home to 54 Chinese carp and 30 or so Mallard drakes and ducks.

In May, the majority of the ducks were up stream, privately hatching their broods. The drakes, their allotted task fulfilled, were lazing round the pond, although the odd one was still wooing and hoping to win. The pond to the sea side is sheltered by a wall and a 10 ft high hedge; to the north stands the hotel, and the remainder is screened by trees some 30 ft high. All attempts to land on the pond into the standard off-shore breeze are tricky, requiring a high approach over the trees, followed by a rapid descent into the turbulence created by the protective hedge, on to a target that is less than 50 yds long.

On the day in question, the off-shore breeze had given way to a force seven gale, which meant that most of the drakes wisely remained grounded. The ducks were otherwise involved. However, in mid-morning, a drake appeared over the trees and was seen to be flying hard into the gale. He dropped like a stone into the shelter of the trees, reduced his now considerable forward momentum with some most dextrous wing work and landed within a yard of the front edge of the pond, veering hard left as he did so to avoid hitting the bank. The safe landing was most skilfully done, but it was a damn near thing.

CG

Moments later, an attempt by a duck was much less masterly and at the very last second she overshot, to be followed immediately by a second duck that suffered a similar fate. Each made two more approaches, trying different techniques, but never managing to beat the tricky wind conditions and always overshooting in good time to clear the hedge. Throughout, the drake looked on anxiously, getting progressively more agitated. After the sixth overshoot, the drake launched himself into the air.

Some two minutes later, a Vic-formation of three appeared, with the drake leading the two ducks. The approach was good considering the conditions and the drake would surely have made it safely; perhaps he was stronger, perhaps his wing area greater, perhaps his power to decelerate was better, but as the round out approached his ladies started to go high on the critical flight path and were in danger of crash landing. The drake saw their problem immediately and he elected to overshoot the formation, guiding it to a safe landing in the sea immediately on the wrong side of the hedge.

Five minutes later, the drake waddled into view, followed by the two ducks. Squawking loudly, they padded across the road, round the trees and along the footpath into the pond. The drake was still very much in command of his small harem, with his swagger and general manner indicating that he was giving a very thorough debrief. Here was a sound lesson for all who fly. In extreme conditions, there had been no dying accidents.

There are obviously some days when a safe approach is impossible. On such days, an alternative safe recovery must be found. We could all learn about flying from that.

I LEARNT ABOUT FRYING FROM THAT

The fact that this incident occurred in the Falklands, on a Tornado F3, has little to do with the tale, except perhaps to add a little through the effect of isolation. Apart from that, it could have been anywhere. The first point to note is that the initial problem, a 'VIB' (engine vibration) caption was just the instigator of events. There we were, somewhere over the flatlands of Lafonia (a bit like Lincolnshire but with more life!) when the aforementioned caption lit up. According to Big Ted's Guide to the F3 - the Aircrew Manual - it meant that the

Panavia Tornado F3

mighty RB199 is leaping around at a rate of many millimetres per second. Lo and behold, if you bring the throttles out of Max War Power (only kidding), the vibration stops and the caption goes out. In accordance with the Flight Reference Cards, the sortie was now over and we returned to Mount Pleasant for an almost normal recovery, for even with one engine at idle all the associated systems were fully functional. However, we had declared an emergency - at least we got that right.

We landed. Now, because this was not really a normal landing in the true sense of the term, the pilot applied the brakes somewhere between a 'tad' and a 'smidgen' early; not too early mind, for the mighty arrestors on the F3 were of a design patented by Raleigh quite some time ago and we are all well aware that the rubber blocks will not take a great amount of punishment. We stopped. We turned. We taxied back. We were unaware as to any problem other than the aforementioned 'VIB' caption, so when ATC asked if we would further require the assistance of the emergency services, we gallantly sent them back home for tea and biscuits. As we arrived at the HAS site, we were met by the Crew Chief with headset lead in hand. We halted (mistake!). We put the parking brake on (bigger mistake!) and signalled for the Crew Chief to come forward. He plugged in and in the language of 'Edsetonian', he said: "Hebbob Dir...I wab toob chayb theb leebbs ober ob theb"...etc etc. This basically meant that he wanted to change the leads on the engine amplifiers to ascertain if the fault was mechanical or electrical. We agreed and awaited his return.

After no more than a minute the Crew Chief came back and asked us to run up the engine in question so as to see if the fault persisted. We did - and it did! He muttered something about a late tea, unplugged his lead and walked off.

The pilot then released the parking brake and ran up the good engine to assist in the final stage of the taxy back, but we did not move. He checked the parking brake was off and tried again. Once again, no joy. "Most odd!" we thought, so a little more power was applied and we heard a creak but no movement. A swift move of the throttle to something just short of minimum afterburner resulted in a loud clunk and we were off. Hard left pedal, a dab of the brakes and throttle to idle took us into the shelter of the revetment where we lined up in front of the HAS.

I shall always remember the look on the face of the one ground crew chap. The easiest way to describe it is as two large white saucers (his eyes) over a large black one (his open mouth) against a chalky white background (his pallor). He was pointing at the starboard wheel and shouting. I couldn't tell you exactly what it was that he said but I do know it had a lot of 'F's in it. I looked over my right shoulder and saw plumes of grey smoke billowing out from under the starboard wing. If one looked closely, one could just discern the heads of the live Sidewinder missiles through it. It was then that all those 'F's began to make sense: "We're on fire", I relayed to my pilot in true crew co-operational style.

The pilot's hands raced madly around the cockpit and as the engines were shut down, the canopy came up. In the face of fire, a radio call was so far down our list of priorities that it was either overleaf or overlooked. In the meantime, I was involved in Aircrew Survival to the extent that I had detached all restraints, straps and blame from the aircraft and stood on my seat. It is funny how your mind works at times, for, with smoke on the right and no ladder on the left, I simply placed my foot on the edge of the cockpit and leapt over the side. After plummeting 10 ft, I hit the ground running and proceeded to give my best impression of Linford Christie, sans lunch box. It was a good 50 m before crew co-operation took hold once more and I looked back at the aircraft. My pilot had also leapt from the pyre but had managed to complete a full forward roll on landing. I now had a complete grasp of the situation, the whole starboard undercarriage was ablaze with flames fanning out over 360º to encompass the pair of missiles under the starboard wing. My 16 years experience of dining-in nights led me to the conclusion that this one... 'was a burner!'

LC

Some time earlier, the pilot and I had noticed that parked outside the ground crew building (but out of view of the HAS in question) was a large fire-engine, the crew of which were carrying out routine checks of a water boiler. With this in mind, both I and the pilot ran on to the taxyway to attract the attention of the fire crew. I was using the universal 'wave' whilst my pilot, more correctly, was using the 'horizontal figure of eight' motion. We actually stood more danger of dying from fatigue than of being run over by a fire engine, for it failed to respond to our frantic gestures. Fortunately, the ground crew chap was rather more on the ball, running into the HAS to reappear with a large fire extinguisher. With the aid of this device, the ground crew extinguished the fire and saved the aircraft (hurrah!).

Meanwhile, up in ATC, a visitor from the 'Bored and Fed-up Section' was watching the proceedings. As with all visitors, he was curious and asked one of the staff, "Is a Tornado supposed to do that?"

"Do what?" asked the Controller.

"Huh!....Wassamarrer....?" asked the Duty Aircrew Officer in the tower.

This was when the flames were at their highest and conversation in the Tower was at its dullest. All hell broke loose. Orders were passed to the fire engine and someone hit the switch that sets off the flashing red lights that signify that the red lights are flashing. The fire engine gunned its motor and roared to the scene of the disaster. All that greeted it was a whisper of smoke and an anti-climax, thanks to the ground crew.

It transpires that the brakes had got hot (obviously) to such an extent that it was the hydraulic oil that had caught fire - hence the recreation of Dante's Inferno. Upon closer inspection, most of the damage was found to be superficial, mainly due to the swift action by those mentioned previously. However, with live weapons on board it could have been a lot worse.

In an office, on a bookshelf, in a manual, somewhere, there is an equation that shows the length of time after application that the brakes will reach their hottest temperature. I assume fire crews know this, for I have often been followed into dispersal by the 'State 2 entourage' who refuse to leave until they have committed the ceremonial laying on of hands upon the wheels of the aircraft to ensure all is well. So, as the Headmaster said at the first assembly after half term, - there are lessons to be learned - for one and all.

HARGEISA OR BUST

The Squadron had been helping to quell a riot in Italian Somaliland. We were stationed at Khartoum and had flown to Mogadishu via Malakal, Juba and Nairobi. There were no modern navigational aids in our Tempest aircraft (at that time we had almost given up hope of even getting a radio compass) and the maps were highly inaccurate. So, it was strictly dead reckoning using equally inaccurate forecast wind speeds and direction. I suffered a considerable number of navigational anxieties on the various 500 to 600 nm legs leading a dozen aircraft - at one stage, Lake Victoria was my one and only hope as a landmark - but we made it.

At the end of the detachment, we were ordered to return via Hargeisa, Khormaksar and Asmara. Between Mogadishu and Hargeisa, there was not one single recognisable landmark on the map, apart from lakes that had long since dried up. Furthermore, we had to fly directly over the Ogaden, which the old sweats will know as 'Goolie' country. Headquarters did their best to help by providing a Mosquito with an expert navigator to guide us. So we all set off.

Perhaps I should have mentioned earlier that one of my flight commanders was due to get married the following week and I was tasked with giving the bride away. After nearly two hours flying, and well over the Ogaden, this particular Flight Commander stopped dreaming of married bliss and called up to tell me that his engine was failing. It finally stopped altogether and I circled with the Squadron to watch him make a forced landing. He seemed to be in one piece and I said a small prayer that he should remain so, knowing this area to be particularly hostile to visitors and bearing in mind the fact that none of us carried 'Goolie chits'.

We again set course with the Mosquito leading and I noted that, by dead reckoning, I had already passed my point of no return. At that moment, the Mosquito's starboard engine failed. It staggered along slowly on one and the pilot said goodbye to us, giving me a course and time to Hargeisa. We continued for another hour or so and passed our estimated arrival time with no sign whatsoever of Hargeisa (the air strip had no aids or radio). At this point, the remaining Flight Commander called to inform me that one of his drop tanks was not feeding and that he had only a few minutes fuel left. I now had frightful visions of the whole Squadron ending up scattered around the desert so I picked a likely flat area and orbited while I thought things out.

First, I tried calling various channels in case anyone might hear me and alert people to our predicament. To my surprise and immense relief, a voice came from a Dakota en route to Khormaksar in which my Group Captain from Khartoum was a passenger. I explained the problem and after a moment's silence my somewhat colourful boss came back with an unusual aid to navigation that I shall always remember. Over the air came this advice: "Look for two hills like women's breasts and Hargeisa is in the middle". I scanned the horizon and, sure enough, visible in the distance were two such objects. We flew towards them, promptly found Hargeisa and all just made it to a safe landing, including the one with so little fuel.

What did I learn? I am still debating that - perhaps it just wasn't my day and perhaps I should never have started, but I am sure Spry has an answer.

Spry's Comment: (*One of my predecessors.....Spry*)

In the circumstances, the first lesson applied was the need to "Keep one's cool". In this story, the formation leader circled a possible forced landing area; he also called for help on all the likely radio channels and sure, they were lucky, but the few resources available were exploited. In today's more sophisticated environment, we tend to take our modern navigation aids for granted and perhaps become a little too complacent. This Tempest pilot had relied extensively on the Mosquito as his nav aid, but it let him down. Although we are now better equipped, electronic gadgets can still go wrong and we could be left as he was, with just a map and a radio. This incident may serve as a timely reminder not to put all our eggs in one basket and to make sure we are briefed upon the best available local information before departure (especially where topographical features are so distinctive!).

GW

A WING MEETING

Canadian CF-101 Voodoo

I was coming to the end of my first year on exchange duties flying the CF-101 Voodoo with 416 Squadron at Chatham in New Brunswick Canada. I had spent the first winter with the OCU in Bagotville, Quebec and so had had about six months on the Squadron. As an ex-Lightning pilot, I was considered experienced in air defence operations and so tended to end up with new, first tour, navigators.

We were taking part in a major annual air defence exercise. We were scrambled at around 0200 hrs against a raid heading in from the Atlantic. For the new navigator, it was his first major exercise and he was understandably keen to do well. However, he was having some problems with his radar and he was unable to get firm lock-ons until quite close ranges. We were armed with the practice Genie nuclear-tipped missile which needed an accurate, recorded, lock-on before firing would count as an MA (mission accomplished).

We were vectored towards a high level target and, because we couldn't get a lock on the front, we ended up in a stern chase. I had advised the Ground Controlled Intercept (GCI) Station that we had some radar problems and requested it to pass accurate ranges as we closed on the target. I also told my navigator that we would break off the attack if he didn't have a firm lock-on at four miles.

GCI called six miles and the navigator said he nearly had it. GCI called five miles, I asked the navigator how things were going, then said I was breaking out. At that exact moment, the target appeared directly ahead and closing fast. I rolled the Voodoo and pulled, but, with the wings vertical, we sliced through the left wing of the target, which was a USAF B-57 Canberra.

The Voodoo began to yaw to the right, while our speed began to fall and I was fully expecting to call ejecting any time. I had put in the after-burners to try and hold some speed - the navigator saw the flash of the burners lighting and shouted that we were on fire. Suddenly, whatever was making us yaw fell off the wing and the aircraft was controllable again. I did a handling check down to about 200 kts and found that one wing began dropping at that speed, so I elected to land at 200 kts plus.

Both aircraft eventually landed at Chatham and both had some very white and shaken aircrew. The B-57 had lost the outer 3 ft of the port wing, together with its outboard fuel tank. We lost the outer 3-4 ft of our starboard wing (not leaving a lot) and had obviously initially collected the B-57 fuel tank and wing. This eventually ripped off the damaged end of my wing, with the tear edge sited only about an inch from the aileron hinge.

Lessons learnt:

✈ Don't press on with a potentially dangerous situation when it's only an exercise.

✈ I was used to flying single-seat and I didn't really appreciate that the young navigator was unhappy with the situation, but that he was pressing on for me and assumed that everything would be all right.

- The ranges I had requested from GCI could not have been expected to be accurate to more than two or three miles in those days.

- The combined altimeter error on the B-57 and the Voodoo had taken out the height difference which should have existed between the fighter and the target.

- The accident rate for exchange officers is, I suspect, higher than for other aircrew. This is because the host service assumes and expects a certain level of expertise and experience, and the exchange officer often may not realise training deficiencies which are relevant to their foreign appointment.

The USAF left their B-57 aircraft parked next to the taxyway at Chatham for about 12 months and it proved a salutary reminder to me every time I flew.

NO MARGIN FOR ERROR

English Electric Lightning

After a three-year tour as a creamed-off QFI, I was posted to the Lightning. I discovered many years later that I had actually been part of an experiment. There was no fast jet pre-OCU training for me on the Hunter - instead, I finished at Leeming one weekend and started the Lightning course at Coltishall the following week. The step from JP to Lightning was steep and I still break out in a cold sweat when I remember my first Lightning solo.

On completion of the course, I was posted to No 5 Squadron at Binbrook. The Squadron was to be the first with the new 'extended range' Lightning Mk3ER which was the forerunner of the Mk6. I was the only one of the core members of the new Squadron who had no previous operational experience. Eventually though, we had enough aircraft and qualified crews to be declared operational. The Louth Standard proudly reported on this event together with a picture of the Squadron members standing alongside the new Lightning with the big fuel tank.

Four days later, a couple of Russian aircraft penetrated the UK Air Defence Region and kept heading south down the North Sea. I was one of the QRA crews that morning and every one got very excited when Q1 was scrambled. Shortly afterwards, as Q2, I was also scrambled and set off with gusto on my first operational mission - this was in the days before we had any air-to-air refuelling support.

Once Q1 had been scrambled, the Russians turned north for home and so I had a long tail chase to catch them. GCI cleared me to go supersonic to catch the intruders, which had now split up. My colleague was shadowing one aircraft which was descending to low level, while the other was also in a shallow descent and I eventually joined it (a Bison) at about 20,000 ft. We continued down. A Lightning F3 appeared from Leuchars, made one pass and headed home, but GCI asked us to continue shadowing for as long as possible.

Once we were low level over the sea, the TACAN broke lock and radio contact with GCI became intermittent. I attempted to establish my position by dead reckoning and monitor the fuel, having used up a fair percentage during the high speed chase. As this was an operational mission and we had been requested to stay with the intruders for as

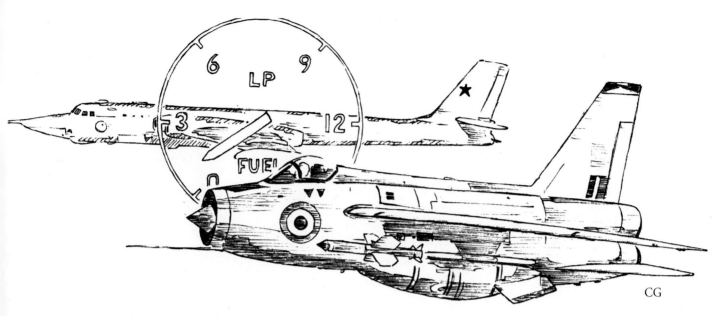

CG

long as possible, I decided I would make a precautionary landing at Leuchars with around 500 lbs a side, rather than the normal minimum landing fuel of 800 lbs a side.

Eventually, I estimated that it really was time to head for an airfield and so I climbed to make radio and radar contact - only to discover I was at least 100 miles further from Leuchars than I had thought. Even at high level, a Lightning used quite a lot of fuel to travel 100 miles and my feverish mental calculations indicated that I would have precious little left on touchdown.

I declared a PAN and remained at high level until more or less overhead Leuchars, then dived with the throttles at idle for the ground. I turned finals with about 300/100 lbs indicating, which wasn't particularly encouraging, for the fuel gauges could be 300-400 lbs inaccurate! Naturally, I breathed a great big sigh of relief when the wheels hit the ground. It was indeed a close call for one engine flamed out by the time I reached the end of the runway and I taxied in dreading that the other one would also fail at any moment.

Lessons Learnt:

The Russians found out a lot more about the Lightning Mk3ER that day than I did about the Bison.

I had left no margin for error. Any minor delay such as a vehicle crossing the runway could have prevented me landing at that moment and would have resulted in the loss of an aircraft. I couldn't even afford to extend the down wind leg.

Whilst it's good to be operational, it is even better to be professional - so don't take foolish risks.

Dead reckoning when manoeuvring at low level in a single seater can be very inaccurate!

English Electric Lightning

IS IT MY TURN TO GRUNT OR AM I WERDLING TODAY?

It was a lovely day for a Gruntwerdle and, as we hoped this was to be the first of a long line of Gruntwerdles, we thought that a good omen. 'We', I should explain, were the members of a fledgling aerobatic team.

As you will realise, this tale is set in high and far-off days - not quite as far back as witches, woodcutters and damsels in distress, but certainly as far back as the time when Porteous manoeuvres were neither spins nor flicks (nor forbidden), when there were more men in the Royal Navy than in the Inland Revenue, and when aerobatic teams sprang up like mushrooms all over the training world.

Our team was different from the rest. The Chipmunk simply hadn't enough power to do formation aerobatics, though we did loop four in line abreast on arrival, because we then had height in hand to sacrifice. So, instead we specialised in synchronised aerobatics. We started as a pair, but after much persuasion allowed two other members of the CNP (Chipmunk Nationalist Party, as we called the Flight) to join us and make a four-strong team.

LC

The new number four proved to be full of bright ideas, some of which even worked. One day, he said, "Surely we don't all have to do the same manoeuvre ..." and out of the ensuing discussion there evolved the celebrated Gruntwerdle.

Do I hear someone asking, "What on earth is a Gruntwerdle?" Imagine four Chipmunks rushing (well, coming) towards each other, two from each end of the airfield. They all pull up, hoping that when they get to the vertical they will be in a straight line at right angles to the display line. From this point, the outside two continue vertically up, while the inside two carry on looping for another 45° of pitch. Then, the leader calls "rudder", at which point the outside two stall turn and the inside two tie a porteous knot in their loops.

That is (or, alas, was) the Gruntwerdle.

What we did not know at this stage was if it would work. There were two particular questions. Firstly, would the outside aircraft fall out of the sky before the inside two were ready? Secondly, could the new pairs get together afterwards? (If you work it out you will see that you change partners in a Gruntwerdle).

The only way to find out was to try it. For safety's sake, we decided to conduct the experiment with only a pair of aircraft. Number two and I would run in together for the first manoeuvre, and that would answer the first question. It would also separate us for a run in to do it again from opposite ends and see if we could join up afterwards. We briefed accordingly and walked out to our aeroplanes watched by an envious number four - after all, it was his idea in the first place.

In those far-off days, there were unused airfields about and we always used one for our practice. (It was legal, even though it wasn't sensible). As we approached Much Binding's old runways, I realised I had not told number two how far out I wanted him. "No sweat," I thought, the spacing we used for the loop at the start of our old pair routine should be just the thing. So I said, "We'll run in as we used to run in for the loop." He promptly acknowledged, moving out to the right distance.

We dived at full power (all 145 horses) and pulled up. I watched number two on my right until the vertical, then looked ahead as I continued looping. At the proper moment, I called "rudder", pulled the stick hard back and put on full right rudder. Earth and sky revolved most satisfactorily - and so did an enormous Chipmunk apparently straight in front of me. It was, of course, my colleague keeping superb station through the loop that my ad hoc 'briefing' had led him to expect. I shall never know how I avoided hitting him, or why he didn't hit me when we were safely down on the ground again. I can only assume he had been carefully brought up. As for the effect it had on our flying, I cannot say, but we certainly learnt about briefing from that.

In case you are wondering, the Gruntwerdle manoeuvre did work satisfactorily, and it became a sort of talisman for us. If you are old enough to remember those days, you will probably recognise the source of the name from the radio programme 'Round The Horne'. Mind you, as Rambling Syd would have said, we never quite worked out which pair was grunting and which pair was werdling. It had to have a name of some kind because I quickly discovered that in synchronised aerobatics the leader needs to call the next manoeuvre all through the sequence. If you rely on the team to remember correctly what comes next, there will inevitably come a day when one of them doesn't. Of course, that's another story, but I learnt about display flying from that, too!

SCOPE FOR DISASTER

Summer time on the Phantom OCU, and in those relatively fuel-economy-free days, flying hours were plentiful and official policy with regard to spare back-seat trips was much more relaxed. Hence, any non-flying types who felt so inclined could put their names down on a list, and sooner or later a slot came up for a back-seat Phantom ride.

Because of the nature of our training task, these slots usually involved air tests (of which there were plenty) and the Navigators' Union was quite happy to give up its seats on what was invariably a boring trip up into the stratosphere. The result was an ideal opportunity to foster relationships with the less fortunate ground-pounders of the base by demonstrating one aspect of the 'sharp end's' operations.

On this particular day, I was detailed to carry out one such air test and, sure enough, the back seat was to be occupied by a simulator instructor. This chap was well known to me, being a pilot on the inevitable ground tour. My immediate reaction was relief at being able to forego the lengthy procedural cockpit, ejection seat and safety equipment brief, as would have been necessary had it been one of the flight-line mechanics. It was an assumption I would live to regret, but right now time was short - and, besides, he was one of us, wasn't he?

We duly kitted up, self-briefed, got some unsuspecting 'wheel' to put his signature in the Authorisation Book and off we went. In the line hut I discovered the air test aircraft was to be a 'two-sticker', a dual control machine used to initiate the fighter pilots into the strange ways of the Phantom. My passenger's reaction was one of delight at the prospect of getting his hands on the pole.

It is worth mentioning that in all other respects, the two-sticker was a normal Phantom, with full radar intercept equipment in the back. The radar scope in the back was in fact an adjustable affair, stowed fully home for take-off and landing, but pulled out once airborne to a more comfortable, parallax-free viewing angle. The significance of this in a two-sticker was soon to be made apparent.

Strap in and start-up were quite normal and trouble free, my passenger being quite happy with the cockpit layout and, pretty soon, we were trundling in fine fashion down to Runway 26.

Line up, cleared for take-off, pressures and temperatures looking good, release brakes and off we go. With reheat engaged, the Phantom wastes no time getting off the ground and the triumph of thrust over aerodynamics was soon manifesting itself as I hit the gear and flap levers. I then prepared, for my passenger's benefit, the 'Saturn 5' reheat climb.

The wheels were just tucking themselves away in the wells at about 100 ft when it happened. The Phantom suddenly pitched up violently. With my heart rate accelerating faster than a Formula 1 racing car, I took the standard recovery action of 'unloading for control'. Simultaneously, the fighter pilot's world famous ultra-rapid scan took in the warning panels - Double Generator failure? Double Power Controls Hydraulic failure? Pitch Stability Augmentation failure? Runway nose up trim? All were guaranteed to produce similar symptoms. While this assessment was going on, the aircraft pitched up again. But all the panels were clear, there were no warning captions, no attention getters, not an amber or red light to be seen anywhere . . . nothing. I had automatically throttled back and now, as we lurched nose up yet again, the speed was bleeding off drastically. All this within the space of a few seconds.

Oh well, I thought, Martin-Baker here we come. As I framed the "Mayday, get the crash crews ready" call in my mind, my thoughts simultaneously turned to getting my passenger out first while I stayed around a bit longer to collect any medals that might be going. It was about then, no more than three to four seconds after the initial pitch up, but seemingly an eternity, that the voice from the back seat spoke up: "Hey, I can't get this radar scope out!" This came at pretty much the same moment I transmitted my "Mayday" call, so the Tower received nothing but a garbled squawk. Their adrenaline levels therefore remained relatively normal as they waited for me to change to Approach, though there may have been some puzzlement over my post-take-off antics.

In the cockpit, the intercom was in danger of melting down as I delivered a short, sharp tirade that consisted mainly of references to my passenger's ancestry and the state of his mental health. The rest of the trip passed in stony, uneventful silence.

The reader will probably have guessed by now what had happened. In those days, the engineers were not in the habit of wire-locking the scopes in the down position when they installed the rear stick for dual flying, mainly because there was a mechanical lock that held the unit down in the first place. In this position, there is about three inches clearance between the base of the rear control column and the radar scope. To withdraw the scope, a lever needs to be depressed and the whole unit then has to be physically pulled out. The engineers quite understandably thought that with the rear stick installed, no-one in his right mind would attempt to withdraw the scope as the results would be traumatic to say the least.

The lesson I learnt? Well, it's easy to look on the phrase 'familiarity breeds contempt' as being a bit of a cliché. But then, so is the saying 'Don't Assume, Check'. The current aircrew knew quite well the rules regarding the rear scope in two-stick Phantoms. My passenger apparently did not and I had failed to brief him.

STALLING FOR TIME

The title "I learnt about flying from that" usually introduces an interesting, and sometimes hilarious episode, in which an aviator recalls a near-fatal mistake from which he has somehow managed to walk away. Many of the tales involve errors of omission: forgot to switch the fuel, will be more careful with cockpit checks in future (perhaps). Mine involved an incorrect action, the consequences of which were not apparent to me at the precise instant, but not long after I literally learned something about flying which I never forgot.

Percival Prentice T1

I joined the RAF around the Korean War period when there was a fair demand for pilots - the intake was heavy and the selectors were not too fussy. I qualified at Hornchurch and was adjudged a reasonable risk for pilot or airgunner training. The fact that I was not recommended for navigator will give some idea of what was thought of my academic potential, as opposed to my ability to move a dot left, right, up or down on a mock TV screen. Reasonable risk I may have been - the fact that I later became a pilot and flew for many years with a fair degree of success proved it. But at the outset, I had at least two handicaps: I was not mechanically minded and I knew nothing about aeroplanes.

My memory may be somewhat vague about this point, but I do not recall learning much more about aeroplanes in Initial Training School because we were mostly far too busy cleaning floors or running around hillsides. And, when I arrived at flying school, ground instruction was concerned more with the insides of engines and the mysteries of meteorological Station Circles than the theory of flight.

My flying began on the Percival Prentice as it happens. I am sure there must be people with fond memories of that aircraft. There must be people with fond memories of Stalin, too, I suppose. Not that the Prentice was a brute or anything, but it certainly wasn't much of an aeroplane.

I managed to solo and slogged on to the BHT, for which my instructor decided to prepare me with one last practice trip. He was an elder flight sergeant with lots of flying time - so much so that the 'creamed-off' instructors used to call him "Sir", I think, or better still he used to call them "Sir" at every opportunity with great relish, particularly when giving them the benefit of his experience - which was quite often.

He had a gentle manner, a soft voice and infinite patience. He explained before the trip that he was going to behave just as a flight commander would on the real handling check, and that I had to be decisive so as to respond positively and act smoothly in the situations I would encounter.

We started with a short take-off. Very soon after I dragged the aircraft into the air in a steep climb, with it hanging on its pathetic matchstick of a propeller, my instructor pulled back the throttle and held it firmly closed. I thought he had gone quite mad, but didn't dare say anything.

"You've had an engine failure . . . what are you going to do?"

I remember his eyes twinkling over his mask as I tried my utmost to prise his hand off the throttle.

"No, no, no", he said. "Do what is to be done".

I looked around desperately for something decisive and positive to do quickly. The undercarriage was fixed, so there was no help there. The engine was clearly out of bounds, and there seemed no point in sending a distress call. Then, I saw the flap lever - that's what he meant! In one smooth movement I grabbed the lever and raised the flap from the take-off position to fully up.

I looked at him hopefully, but his eyes had ceased to twinkle; they actually seemed to frown as he said: "Wrong".

It takes more time to write about the incident than it took to happen in reality, but, even after all these years, it seems that time passed very slowly, as we fell like a stone towards the earth. During those anxious moments, my instructor gave me the lesson in aerodynamics that I feel I should have had elsewhere, ideally in a classroom and long before this event. He told me that raising the flap had effectively reduced our wing area and that we were stalling.

"You do know what a stall is, I trust?" he enquired.

"Yes Sir, do you have control?"

He had, but somewhat late, as seconds afterwards the aircraft struck the ground with a great slap, and hangars and control towers passed dizzily across my vision 'til the silence came. His voice was still soft, but he didn't meet my eye as he busied himself turning off switches and unfastening his harness.

"5000 hrs, not a blemish, not a scratch. A1 instructor, Command IRE, Master Green (Instrument Rating) - then you. Tell me, what now do you know about flaps?"

I learnt about high lift devices from that!

OUT OF CONTROL - ON THE GROUND!

GW

A Victor tanker scramble, while being hard work for the crew, was generally a relatively leisurely procedure because there was usually a fair distance to travel from the 'line' to the runway. This taxy time offered opportunities to double-check that nothing had been missed and to complete the pre-take-off checks, so that having reached the marshalling point one could call for line-up and immediate take-off. On one occasion, however, we were flying from a FOB and the aircraft had been parked on the ORP at the end of the runway. The full impact of this didn't sink in until it was nearly too late.

We had been flying together as a crew for some time and we naturally thought ourselves to be pretty good. We certainly believed we could get a Victor off the ground faster than just about anyone else.

On this particular evening, we were just coming to the end of our stand-down period. We were sitting in the Mess having a quiet Coke and chatting up some of the local 'talent' when the Detachment Ops Officer stuck his head round the door and shouted "Scramble". We immediately told him that we were not due to come up to 60 minutes readiness for another five minutes, that we were not even changed, and that he could put his scramble in a very painful place. He was adamant that it wasn't a joke and that we were 'the only crew available'. We left the ante-room in some confusion, sprinted to our rooms, changed into our immersion suits and then ran to the front of the Mess where the crew-coach was waiting. As we shot through the foyer, we shouted a quick goodnight to the girls, one of whom was heard to comment, "Cor - isn't it exciting; just like something from an Alistair Maclean novel". We had obviously impressed them - something we had been trying unsuccessfully to do all evening.

After a short but hair-raising drive we reached the aircraft, I scribbled in the Form 700 and we started to get the show on the road. We strapped in and while the Plotter was closing the door and removing the ejection seat pins, the Co-pilot and I started the engines. After-start checks were soon completed and, because we were already effectively at the marshalling point, I called for take-off. I taxied on to the runway, checked the brakes at 88% and, applying full power, roared off down the runway. A quick look at my watch told me we had taken 14 minutes from the Mess in civvies to rolling down the runway fully kitted-up, which was not bad, not bad at all.

Everything was going well and I started to relax a little.

We were approaching 100 kts and accelerating fast when the Air Engineer said, "Are we taking-off?"

"Yes, why?" I asked.

"The bloody flying controls are not on!" he yelled back at me.

Sheer panic! In less time than it takes to tell, the Co-pilot and I reached out and flicked the required 10 switches up and we were immensely relieved to see the power failure warning lights go out. By this time, we had passed rotation speed and the end of the runway was approaching fast. But, now that we had flying controls, it was a simple matter to lift the aircraft off the ground.

I had heard of others trying to get airborne without the controls being switched on but I never for a moment thought it could happen to me - how wrong I was. We had missed not just one check, but a whole check list. Nothing about the events of that evening was ever said outside the crew, loyal bunch that they were. However, my professional pride had been severely dented and I felt I ought to say something about it to somebody - but who? I was tempted to submit a 'CONDOR' but it was a new procedure then and I was not sure if it could be trusted. I know now that the guarantee of confidentiality is cast-iron and that I should have reported the incident. Even now, every time I remember racing down the runway without flying controls my mouth goes dry and a cold shiver runs down my spine.

I certainly learnt about flying from that!

Handley Page Victor

75

SUIT YOURSELF

Many years ago, I was just completing my first tour on AEW Shackletons at Lossiemouth. As with all things in life, it was necessary to keep current and here follows the tale of a sea drill that probably had Davy Jones rolling in his locker.

Spring had sprung and the sea temperature had risen sufficiently to permit immersion suits to be cast off with a degree of abandon. Sea Drill time arrived and the eight nominees and I rooted around in their lockers for the bunny suits and woolly-pullys that had last seen light of day some twelve months earlier - during the last sea drill in fact. Once fully dressed and resembling a crowd of Michelin men, we awaited the CSRO so that we could don the 'drill' immersion suits and be on our merry way. However, we had failed to take into account the fact that the CSRO had a problem with his back - there was a mean streak running down it. Upon his arrival, we (the willing) were informed by him (the warm) that as it was normal policy not to wear immersion suits on routine sorties, then he could see no reason for us to wear them for the drill. His logic was that the sea temperature was ten degrees, which was legal, and that was that! What a jolly jape we thought - but he was serious. With pallors paled and pupils glazed, we made our way to the awaiting coach like Christians with 'Eat me' labels attached!

The weather was reasonable for the time of year. It was a bit windy and overcast, but at least it wasn't raining. The coach trip was made in silence as we attempted to retain precious warmth. A short wait at the quayside of some remote Scottish harbour saw all nine victims huddled behind a wall for shelter, whilst the CSRO stood at the end of the jetty, beckoning to the safety boat, in a scene taken straight out of 'The Flight Lieutenant's Woman'. All possibilities, including sinking, scurvy and even mutiny, were discussed but we finally resigned ourselves to the fact that it was a futile gesture. We were going to get wet, no question about that.

As the waves washed over the bow of the boat, fear washed over the eight and I. We all felt the cold cut through the layers of clothing, all except the CSRO who was wrapped up warmer than a haemorrhoid in a spacesuit. It was about now that things started to happen. The co-pilot, who was nicknamed 'The Ninestone Cowboy' due to his stature and lack of natural padding, started to babble a bit. However, he always did this so it was not until his symptoms progressed that we were able to ascertain he was coming down with hypothermia before he had even left the boat! He was taken below, as they say in naval terms, and his name was deleted from the list. Then there were eight.

The engines cut and the boat slowed to a rhythmical bob. The CSRO stood astern of the boat like Captain Ahab, dinghy in one hand and guard rail clip in the other. The seven and I donned lifejackets and formed up at the back of the boat. We were to simulate a belly landing in the Shackleton, followed by a wingtip entry into the dingy that would automatically deploy on impact - what could be simpler? If we disregarded the fact that the Shackleton chin radome had the water-skiing characteristics of an open skip, and if we ignored the fact that the only two survivors of a Shackleton ditching were both sat in the galley when the back end of the aircraft disappeared from around them, and if we also took no notice of the time that the 'Wing Mounted Dinghy Activation System' failed completely when it was set off as a confidence boosting measure one ground training day, then the scenario seemed feasible. With morale plummeting like a miner's lift, we gathered our thoughts.

"I'm antrim" mumbled the Flight Engineer, who was behind me in the queue to disembark.

"What was that?" I asked, more out of politeness than interest.

"I can't swim," he stated, with a look that was probably similar to that of Captain Oates when he said he was 'just popping out'.

Splash!!!..... Hissssss..... the dingy was in the water and inflating. Naturally, it was the wrong way up. The Captain had been nominated as the first man in, since he was the biggest and the strongest and the bravest (all that was decided in the last 30 seconds). He pleaded that he really should be the last to board as he would remain 'wrestling' with the controls until the final moment. In response, we insisted that he would in fact leave that job to the Co-Pilot and, since the Co-pilot was absent, missing presumed chilled, his plea held little water, unlike his boots in two minutes time.

The Captain relented, took a mighty leap into the water and disappeared below the briny, only to bob up again a second or so later imitating Duncan Goodhew on fast forward. He swam to the dinghy, grabbed the strop that ran along the bottom and hauled the inflatable over like a man possessed. If there was a record time for righting and boarding a dinghy, he had just shattered it - he was big, he was strong, he was brave... he was bloody frozen!

Whilst watching the Captain's heroic struggle, I conferred with another crew member as to what to do with the Flight Engineer. We agreed to sandwich him between us to ensure he would be OK. The queue in front was there no longer; there was mayhem in the water as people thrashed about wildly in an attempt to emulate the Almighty and walk to the dinghy. I peered over the edge of the boat, inflated my lifejacket, felt the CSRO prizing my fingers from the guard rail and began to count myself in.... One..... Twarghhhhh!! I was pushed! I felt the overwhelming cold as the water enveloped me completely. The only breath in my body vacated the premises for warmer climes, leaving me gasping for breath. It was like sitting under a sprinkler whilst undressing in an industrial freezer. All rational thought disappeared. Drills! What drills? All I wanted was to be in that dinghy before I died. At last I could see blue sky, at last I could breath; at larghhgle glug gluggle - the Flight Engineer landed on top of me. What seemed like several hours later, I finally surfaced, to discover that the dinghy was at least several miles away. I swam towards it with a gusto hitherto unknown....and all the time I was trying to get my breath.

"Here's one," cried the Captain in the dinghy to his fellow boarder.
I tried to convey to them that the Flight Engineer was in greater need as he could not swim.

"Ghet thhhhhooo Enghhhhhinnhhherr," I gulped, attempting to speak.

A puzzled look flickered across the Captain's face.

"Thhhheeee Eng cahhhhnnnnnnt wimmnmm!" I gulped again.

There was no sign of comprehension from the crew of the dinghy. I attempted to compose myself - it was the Engineer's only hope.

"Thhhheee Enggg cahhhnnnt wimmmmm" I cried.

"Quick! Get Ken - he's in real trouble!" yelled the Captain.

I felt two pairs of hands grab my life jacket and haul me aboard, for which I must admit I was truly grateful. With a face full of rubber floor and an aircrew boot in my ear, my relief was cut short by the realisation that the Flight Engineer was still out there. I managed to right myself and peer out only to see the poor fellow drifting off in the general direction of the Faroes.

After much deliberation, we managed to haul the bodies in and conducted a head count. Seven?.... we counted again.... Seven! One was missing! Then and only then did we hear the strains of a whistle being blown at the decibel equivalent of the QE2's hooter. We dropped the door cover and, sure enough, there was the simulated casualty bobbing around, whistling like a demented kettle, waving frantically and freezing.
A debate then ensued as to who should go and get him, the request for volunteers having fallen on frozen ears. The Captain got a grip of the situation and nominated someone, only to be informed in no uncertain terms that sex and travel were the order of the day. All were then nominated in turn and all had sundry excuses, ranging from injuries sustained in the boarding to having to arrange their CDs in alphabetical order! At this point, the dinghy bobbed down, followed by a cry which cast grave doubt over the marital status of the parents of those on board the dinghy. It was a

miracle! The casualty had fully recovered in the time that we were debating his plight - for he had become so cold waiting for rescue that he thought it better to abandon the idea of pretending to be a casualty before he became one for real. We hauled him on board - at last we were eight. We bailed out, we swore at each other, we simulated taking sea sickness pills, we swore at each other, we said we were cold and we all swore at each other.

After running out of profanities and expletives, we were hauled alongside the safety boat, taken aboard and sent below to change. We stayed below, for it was the warmest place that side of the 12 nm limit. We whiled away the time by plotting the demise of the CSRO. Throwing him overboard was the outright winner, though it was followed closely by the idea of slitting his throat before throwing him overboard.

As with all stories, there is a moral. The rules say 10° is the limit but that is not warm by any stretch of the Lycra shorts. In subsequent years, I became very reluctant to doff my immersion suit until the warmth of the sun on my back made heat exhaustion a very real alternative. In fact, one year, I wore my 'goon' suit all through a British summer which more resembled a mild extended winter. I do not suggest that we should all leap into the sea when it reaches 10°, but what I do recommend is that we take a few seconds to think about how cold we would be, for how long, and how we could prevent that for the sake of a little effort. Immersion suits will keep you warm - but not if they are on the peg in Flying Clothing!

LC

ALL FIRED UP

A few nights ago, immersed in the mood of dejection and weariness that so often assails the MOD commuter about mid-week, I was reminiscing about the Rhodesian towns and villages I had known well on cross-country flights over 25 years ago when I was learning to fly.

The memory of one particular night came flooding back. I was in the dimly lit cockpit of a Harvard, in which I nervously awaited clearance to take off on my first night solo. By now, I had flown about 70 hrs, mostly on Tiger Moths. I had sat in a Tiger on the edge of Heany strip watching the more advanced courses in their bright yellow Harvards come rasping in to land at what looked like incredibly high speeds. And, in due course, I had progressed.

Never again would an engine fill me with quite such awe as when the Pratt and Whitney Wasp first roared into life in front of me, all 600 hp shaking and rattling the aircraft with terrible fury. My course had soloed by day, had stalled and spun, had lost one or two on the way and now the time had come to try our hands at night. Like most pilots on their first night solo, I was a touch apprehensive and perhaps not without reason. Earlier that evening, after several dual circuits which varied only in degree of ineptitude, my instructor had departed, somehow satisfied with my performance. And so, I slung my parachute over my shoulder and trudged out on my own.

The green light flashed. I taxied on to the flarepath, carefully aligning the single line of lights along the left-hand side of the cowling before I opened up. The usual swing, tail up, lights speeding by, airborne! Brakes on, undercarriage up, increase the speed for the climb. The flarepath fell behind and I ascended into the inky black African night. Ahead, the ground was devoid of light except for the occasional flicker of a Bantu fire; above, countless stars looked down with a brilliance seldom seen outside the tropics. I began to relax.

As my eyes adjusted to the darkness, I became uncomfortably aware of a dull red glow on the right-hand side of the nose. Curious, I leaned over and looked out. An appalling sight met my eyes. A sheet of white hot flame spur

from the engine cowling, passing inches below the canopy rail and apparently enveloping the whole of the starboard side of the fuselage. Aghast, I checked the other side - exactly the same. The whole aeroplane was ablaze! I am not ashamed to admit that I was paralysed by fear. Too low to bale out, a forced landing in the rocky void below quite unthinkable. What could I do? Call for help? Not for the last time, I found that transmitting a coherent, calm message when one is petrified with fear, calls for a considerable effort of will, which, at that time, was quite beyond me.

I waited anxiously for the explosion which I knew would come at any moment to scatter the remains of the Harvard and me over the ground below. I tried rationalising : "The b.... thing can't be on fire, it's just not possible on your first night solo on type!" Less than a year later, I would know better (but that's another story). However, in my then unspoilt ignorance, my self-deception brought me some comfort. The aircraft still flew. Nonetheless, my burning desire (*groan....Spry*) was to return to earth as fast as I could.

Hurriedly I turned downwind, settling lower in the seat and resolutely refusing to look over the side, though the ominous glow persisted. The wheels hung down and I turned on to finals, still far too fast and quite high. Full flap, throttle back, but I was coming in much too fast. I felt for the ground and, with an almighty crash, found it. Eventually, we careered to a stop. Looking back on half a lifetime of landings of varying degrees of mediocrity, that particular arrival still stands out as the perfect example of all that a landing should never be. Still, the main thing was that I was down in one piece. Sweating and panting, I turned off the landing strip, applied the brakes and quickly began to unstrap.

It was then that I noticed the red glow had subsided - in fact it seemed to have disappeared completely. Peering out of the cockpit, I could see no sign of fire. What on earth?! Gingerly, I opened the throttle - a great spout of flame spurted from the exhausts. I closed the throttle: the flames retreated whence they came. Years later, someone mentioned to me that some Harvard exhausts were shielded for night flying while others weren't! What a clown I was! But that was not the end of it...

NA Harvard

I began the after landing checks, my heart still pounding madly. Trimmers to neutral, flap up... No sooner had I raised my left hand than I realised my mistake. I looked down; sure enough, my left hand was grasping the undercarriage lever in the raised position. I sat aghast, waiting for the propeller to churn into the ground, but nothing happened. Behind me, my fellow students continued their circuits and bumps, oblivious to my predicament. Cautiously, I lowered the lever and raised the one next to it. The flaps retracted. Tentatively, I released the brakes and the aircraft rolled forward. Thank God for the geometric lock!

So what did I learn that night? First, that I was not infallible. This fairly comes as a great shock when one realises it for the first time, since we all believe it to be so, despite all the evidence to the contrary. I didn't learn much else at that time, but later however, experience added emphasis to one or two points which emerged in retrospect.

Perhaps the most important lesson was that no matter what the emergency, it is often the best policy to do absolutely nothing until one has had a chance to mentally size up the situation. That may seem obvious, but time and time again in later years I was to see that more harm can be done by the instant panic reaction to an emergency than may already exist; better to grit one's teeth and take deliberate, considered and correct action.

So, after an emergency, when you've got that dry feeling in the mouth and a wet feeling in your flying gloves, consciously stop and make yourself think before you take any action. Should your hand be on that switch? Is that LP cock really the one you want to switch off? Don't do it until you are certain you are right. And don't forget to check your actions afterwards in the flip cards - the chances are that you will have forgotten something important.

Finally, remember that from time immemorial aircraft designers have felt honour bound to install an ambiguous switch, an easily misread instrument or a confusing lever with the express purpose of humbling the fools who mistreat their precious creations. Watch out for design flaws in the aircraft you fly regularly, and especially in the ones you fly less regularly, because they are mistakes waiting to happen.

METEORIC DOWNFALL

When other reasons for an accident are difficult to find, it is sometimes useful for the Board of Inquiry to check if the pilot knew someone who lived near the scene.

This goes back a long way in aviation lore. I was reminded of it recently by reading 'Spitfire on my Tail' by Ulrich Steinhilper, a Battle of Britain Me 109 pilot. At his flying school near Berlin in 1937, pupils had many accidents on solo cross-countries. Steinhilpes wrote: "Recognising that it was the unscheduled aerobatics which caused most of the fatal accidents, our instructors tried to limit our games. They soon realised that many accidents had taken place in the vicinity of a pupil's parents', girlfriend's or relative's home. The cause was apparent - showing off. Soon they had a register of all 'significant sites' for the pupils and training routes were designed to avoid this kind of temptation".

I got a lesson about this myself, when I was a young sprog learning to fly Meteors. One day a full ventral tank at last put my home within reach by air. There was not much time to divert and get back to what I was supposed to be doing, so I set off at low level with the old 'Meatbox' on the 'blue note' which they gave at full chat. There was stratus at about 1800 ft and I was doing 400 kts just underneath it. Having just come off comparatively slow pistons, I had little idea of g-loads at that speed. As the scenery shot past, I banked steeply trying to pick out my old school. Pulling too hard and looking back over my shoulder at the same time, I blacked myself out with no trouble at all. It only lasted a moment, but when I was able to see again, I was in cloud with all the instruments winding round rapidly in opposite directions. Since my instrument flying was quite unequal to the situation, my immediate reaction was to push the stick forward sharply so as to get below cloud again. The resultant negative g showered me with ancient crud from the floor, but worse, instantly gave the sensation of being upside down. I rolled hard, but kept pushing the stick in case the ground was above my head, thus becoming even more disorientated, if such a thing was possible. I cannot confirm the old cliché about your whole life passing before your eyes, but I can distinctly remember thinking: "You bloody fool, you've really done it this time." This was accompanied by a strong desire to be somewhere else - anywhere else - at that particular moment.

Fortunately, the aircraft suddenly shot out of cloud in a shallow dive and all was well. I proceeded very gently back to base, shaking like a leaf. Whether any of the half million people underneath had been impressed I do not know, but I somehow doubt it.

The Meteor was having a lot of accidents at this time, with sensational press coverage. Diving into a crowded Woolworths would not only have done me little good personally, but it would have been fairly awkward for the RAF as well.

In my subsequent flying career, I did many things, but showing off again over a girlfriend's house was not one of them

WHEN I WAS ON.....

Many years ago, I was learning to fly the JP. As part of the course, we all had to complete a solo landaway and, due to a stunning piece of planning, four students all ended up going to Valley on the same day at the same time. During the turnround, we decided it would be a good idea to do a bit of illegal close formation on the way back and so three of us joined together in Vic formation during the transit home. I was in echelon starboard on my fellow student leader when all of a sudden we were presented with a plan view of another JP going vertically upwards in front of us and missing us by a very small margin

Jet Provost T.3A

indeed. It was, of course, the fourth student who'd planned to do the pull up in front of the Vic, but who totally mistimed it and nearly wrote off four aircraft in the process. That evening, four very chastened students huddled together in the corner of the bar and discussed how ill-advised their actions had been.

A year or so later, I was training to be a fighter pilot. This entailed flying the Hunter at the then equivalent of the TWU and having a thoroughly good time. There was quite intense competition between those of us going to Lightnings and those staying on the Hunter. Naturally, this competition extended to all aspects of life - including flying. In the air-to-air range there was an island (let's call it Puffin Island) which had a lighthouse sited just off the southern tip with enough space to squeeze a Hunter through between the lighthouse and the actual island. On one occasion, I and another student departed the target flag simultaneously. He dived down towards Puffin Island and I set off in hot pursuit - after all, he was going to Hunters and I was going to Lightnings. It became obvious he was going for the gap and there was no way I was going to chicken out. As he went though, I was about 400 yds behind, arriving at the gap just in time to be confronted by a huge flock of birds his aircraft had disturbed into flight. About 10g later, I recovered from the subsequent vertical climb and was very lucky not to have had a multiple bird strike which could easily have taken out the engine.

Eventually I arrived on my first squadron to fly the Lightning. This was not an aircraft noted for its great range, since it carried less than 8,000 lbs of fuel (without extra-large ventral tanks) and had a total thrust in excess of 32,000 lbs with the burners lit. I soon discovered that the old hands on the Squadron seemed to do longer sorties than me, so what was the secret? It all became clear one happy hour, when I learned that the aircraft could fly comfortably on one engine (in fact you hardly noticed), so why not transit to and from the play area with the number two shut down?

Hawker Hunter

On the following Monday, off I went to transit with just one engine running. I got into the practice intercepts and relit the second engine, or at least tried to relight it but it wouldn't start for some reason. I wondered what to do - whether to go home and admit I'd closed down the engine (against ASIs, but who read them anyway?) or just keep quiet about it? I completed the sortie on one engine, taxied in very gently and shut down without telling anybody. Sure enough, on the next sortie, the number two engine would not start. Nothing untoward you may feel, but a few years later we lost a Lightning for exactly the same reason. It was loitering on one engine, the other wouldn't restart and, during the relight attempts, pooled fuel exploded and the aircraft was consequently lost. I must have been lucky that day.

And now, pilot heaven, flying the Lightning in Germany, mostly at low level, and 'unbriefed affiliation' (low level combat) with the whole of the Second Allied Tactical Air Force (2ATAF) was the order of the day. The Lightnings often used to run into German G-91s from Ahlhorn and some ding-dong fights ensued, for both aircraft could turn extremely well.

Anyway, everyone in 2ATAF used to go to the peat cuttings in Low Flying Area 1, which was as flat as a pancake for miles with the highest obstruction being the crane that cut the peat. Inevitably, everybody had to see how low they could really fly, didn't they? I found myself up there on my own one day performing one of the old Low Level Search Patterns. Down as low as possible, speed a moderate 360 kts but eyes very firmly ahead so as not to hit the crane if it appeared. Out of the corner of my eye, I caught a glimpse of a tailplane on top of a fin and then an F-104 Starfighter crossed my nose at about 50 yds range and about 10 ft below my height - he must have been following a dyke, otherwise his belly would have been on the ground. Presumably he, like me, was eyes rigidly ahead with nil lookout; how we missed each other goodness only knows. As a matter of interest, about that time an aircraft from the other Squadron came back with a tree stuck in the ventral fuel tank. The pilot claimed he was tired, had fallen asleep at low level and woke up just as he was about to hit the tree. He got away with it as well!

Some years later, I was pottering around as a Bulldog QFI and had to ferry an aircraft to another station on a day when the weather was not too good. As usual, we had no navigation aids whatsoever and so I had to stay VFR as I transited civilian controlled airspace. To cut a long story short, I followed various coastlines and popped across sundry stretches of water - not illegal at 500 ft but there was absolutely no where to go if the engine quit, for there were no beaches in this part of the world. When I arrived at my destination, I broke into the circuit and, unlike a jet, in a Bulldog you apply full power at the break. I duly did, whereupon the engine promptly threw a big end or something in a spectacular fashion. I managed to make the runway but little else. I don't believe anybody's had to ditch a Bulldog yet but I must have been fairly close to it that day.

And now to the F-4. I'd always been good at instrument flying and had been an instrument rating examiner on every

English Electric Lightning

Bulldog

type I'd flown. We're on a simple GCA back into base, as a singleton, with the weather not too bad and absolutely nothing to do but fly the aircraft. All of a sudden, the pedal shaker starts, coupled with a strangled shout from Vasco in the back - the nose is 15° up in the air and the angle of attack is very, very high and still going up. I recover the situation and then complete the GCA. What went wrong stemmed from pure inattention. My mind was in neutral, I was not concentrating on a simple task and we nearly got into bother. Mind you, as Vasco later admitted, he was switched off as well and should really have been monitoring things much more closely.

Have I learnt throughout the years? Yes, of course I have, but things can still go wrong. Taxying out the other night, the student in the front seat gave me control so I could check my brakes from the back. The left brake was OK, but the right brake went flat to the floor with no response and the aircraft continued turning inexorably left towards the grass. I shouted to the student but that was no good, because my mask was dangling at the end of its chain instead of being on my face, and he couldn't hear a thing. Then I really knew about one-armed paperhangers. I managed to get the mask up, switch the microphone on and shout a warning to him just in time to prevent a very embarrassing interview with the Station Commander.

So, I've had my share of little incidents, any one of which could have put me into an early grave. Fortunately, I've been lucky and I'm still around to talk about them - but a lot of my contemporaries are not. I've certainly learnt about flying over the years; but even now, it's still quite easy to get caught out.

IDLE CHATTER COSTS

Over the years I have enjoyed the recollections of all those who have contributed to 'I Learnt About Flying From That'.

In my own career, I had one fortunate escape, but was less sure if I could say I had learnt about flying from that. I wondered if I could identify a similar situation where my actions, based on earlier experience, were correct and where problems which arose were dealt with logically and without a significant increase in the flow of adrenaline? In fact, I have had such an experience and, since it had a mildly humorous ending (at the time, as well as in retrospect), I decided it might be worth relating to show how a little practical learning and acquired wisdom can sometimes make all the difference to the end of a sortie.

Phantom F-4

DH 115 Vampire T11

It began when I was nominated to be a member of a Board of Inquiry into a helicopter accident near Kuala Lumpur, although since I was then flying Venoms, I was mystified as to what profoundly useful contribution I could make. The Board was due to adjourn at lunchtime on Saturday and I had arranged for a Vampire to collect me and return to Singapore. I duly climbed aboard, having been to the Met Office, Flight Planning and Movements to ensure that no unpleasant surprises were likely to be lurking en route and that everyone who needed to know was aware I was coming. Basically, I was double-checking, although I hoped the incoming pilot had done the right things as well. The fairly standard probability of thunderstorm cloud was the only possible cause for concern but not to the extent that it should impede our progress, especially on a Saturday lunch time.

We set off in the Vampire T11 and cruised along at medium level, going through all the correct frequencies and ultimately being handed over to Tengah. The thunderstorm clouds were there as forecast, but, with the aid of Tengah ATC to get us down, they did not seem too intimidating. The picture soon changed, however, as at the handover stage from Singapore Centre to Tengah Approach the radio went completely dead. We tried every frequency, only to be greeted by total silence. Although we were calling Tengah, we had hoped there might be some response from someone, somewhere, but it was as if the whole ATC branch had brought down the shutters and adjourned to the bar. As time was getting on, it was a philosophy with which we whole-heartedly agreed, although we would have preferred them to get us on the ground first.

It was now that my previous and relatively recent experience came to mind. Since an earlier event, I had boned up on range and endurance to the extent that I knew what heights and speeds to fly, I knew how far we could go and how long we could remain in the overhead until it was necessary to return to Kuala Lumpur. Since I was confident that Kuala Lumpur would remain open, both in terms of weather and people in the tower, it was therefore with an easy mind that I discussed with my colleague the various options before us, including the decision not to try any of the other island airfields in view of the thunderstorm activity.

Having completed this mind-clearing exercise, there was still time to cruise around looking for a hole over Tengah before heading back north, for I knew that it was unwise to descend without a clear sign of the airfield and without ATC assistance! There was also time to chat about life at Tengah, in all its forms and activities. Young officers always know how best to run any size of outfit, certainly up to station level. It is only when they gain responsibility that they learn life is never quite as straightforward as it seems and we were no different. We did, of course, also comment on the gross dereliction of Air Traffic in leaving us to cope with such a predicament and pondered upon how they could do such a thing, bearing in mind the good relationship which existed between the Controllers and the Squadron.

It was a break in the clouds which turned our minds from an undoubtedly fascinating and wide-ranging debate to consideration of a free descent. There was more good fortune as we saw part of the airfield and that it was dry. We descended without difficulty and entered the circuit knowing we were past the last landing time for normal Saturday operations and thus there would be no conflicting traffic. However, we were both slightly surprised when a green verey flare rose from ATC at an early stage in our descent, but it encouraged us to continue our approach from which we duly landed and taxied in, with plenty of time to make the bar.

It was good of so many people to come down and see us in. Some of them were quite senior, and wouldn't normally turn out to meet two fairly junior officers, but judging by their smiling expressions they were apparently happy to see us safely back. We were invited to change and meet for a drink in the Mess. We did just that - only to find that we were paying. Yes, you've guessed it - from the time we first called Tengah we were stuck on transmit! However, as far as the professional side was concerned, the calculations made and the decisions taken had been perfectly correct and for that I think we were duly complimented. Furthermore, our peripheral conversations had not caused offence, although we were both hard put to recall what and who we might have discussed.

I like to think it was my previous experience which had made me do the necessary homework to ensure that in similar circumstances I would not be caught out again - and I am happy to say that in this instance, such was the case. However, I did insert into the memory box the fact that radio silence, while possibly golden, may only be a one-way thing - and that while you may not be able to hear them, it is quite conceivable that they can hear you!

STRAFE STREWTH

Picture the scene. Very early in the 1980s, a chap was on his first tour on a single-seat strike attack squadron in Germany with a motto of 'Facta non Verba'. Loosely translated this means 'Deeds not Words', except of course on the stats board where it was written backwards! No more clues given.

Arriving in November, by mid-summer of the following year, I was operational and enjoying the delights of four or five days per month on 'Q'. I was also beginning to feel both confident and competent in both of the Squadron's assigned roles. One hazy sunny day, the Ground Liaison Officer appeared in the crewroom with a short-notice task. "The engineers are doing some bridging on the Weser and are looking for some over-flights and attacks. Any takers?" Well, it seemed silly not to and it would nicely fill in the three hours until the pubs opened. Banter duty 'auth' to obtain aeroplane and trusty number two - or in this case, two of them - two pairs leaders to fly together in a Jaguar T2. Plan, brief and launch. All going well so far. The engineers were supposed to be bridging at two sites, so the plan was to level overfly both, followed by a planned strafe re-attack against both. The strafe attacks were correctly planned and the brief included pull-up points and minimum speeds for each part of the manoeuvres.

It was a classic, murky, sunny, North German plain afternoon and all went as planned up to the first bridging site where nothing was seen. We continued to the second site, with number two in trail and simulated dropping eight cluster bombs on the bridging, which was positioned exactly as advertised. Extend, turn, check speed, check number two, round the village, abeam the church, pull up, tip over and down into the dive. Acquire. Track...Track...Track. Fire! Recover (not below 500 ft agl), level, extend, turn round the wood, cross the pylons, pull up for site one, speed OK, down the dive. Still nothing seen...Look...Hunt... No good, recover.

As I levelled off, there was a frantic call from the number two's back seat of "400 metres west in the trees". Right, thinks I, they're not getting off that easily! Call "re-attacking right". Pull hard to the right, max dry thrust, pull up, tip in, Speed? No time to look at trivia like that.

Looking... Looking... Looking. Suddenly, there they are. Yug to the left. Adjust. Sight on. Track. Fire! God, the trees are looking big. Height 400 ft, nose 15º down. Speed about 340 kts. Pull! No, relax, get the burners lit... Nozzles opening... Now pull to the nibble... Must not over-pull... Hit the flap lever... Flaps travelling... Aircraft responding... Nose coming up... Trees on either side of cockpit and peripheral impression of lots of waving soldiers who seem to think the show is for their benefit!

Cancel reheat, raise flaps, level at 2000 ft. "Two where are you?" Long silence ensues and then number two checks-in, having gone to guard in anticipation of the Mayday call. Fly home in silence. Land and sign-in. "Chief, can you have a quick look at the flaps, I might have overstressed them a bit". Debrief with now not so trusty number two and then buy the first two rounds as a penance.

What did I learn? Off-range strafe is always potentially dangerous, especially in a heavily-laden or high wing-loading aircraft like the Jaguar. It must always be properly planned and should never be done 'off the cuff', however tempting the prospects might be. What upset me most of all though was that it never even crossed my mind to eject. That would have been to admit pilot error and I was far too good for that. I hope that I now know I'm not quite as good as I think I am and that even the best sometimes make mistakes.

As a postscript, the flaps were not damaged and I got a pat on the head from the Boss in response to a very complimentary signal of thanks from the engineers. However, I did think the bit about realistic training and the thunderous roar of jet engines was going a bit far.....

GW

NIBBLED TO DEATH BY DUCKS

Panavia Tornado GR1A

After 15 years of flying with a scepticism that would make Thomas seem a fanatical believer, how could I have ended up with full left stick, at 200 ft and in a gentle roll to the right? Well, to paraphrase that great military mind General Melchett, a total pig-headed unwillingness to look facts straight in the face helped.

The deployment had not gone to plan. Because of air transport problems, the first eight Tornados to arrive were seen in by the previous visiting squadron, who just that morning had waved their own aircraft off. I arrived the following day with two more aircraft and was told that the advance party would turn up that evening at about the same time as the main party! Repairs to the main runway meant that the groundcrew changeover took place ten miles down the road, so the engineering handover was fairly abbreviated. The ducks were just beginning to nibble!

Then along came a monstrous mallard. For urgent operational reasons, two of the original eight aircraft had to return to base the next day with full underwing fuel tanks. With only limited manpower (one man who, having unwisely holidayed nearby, was surprised to arrive at work to find he represented the entire engineering infrastructure) and little equipment, only refuelling and turnround were possible. The underground-fed refuelling pantographs were convenient but ungauged (Quack).

The sun rose on a frustrated team, in part comprising tired engineers, augmented by tense aircrew off home early and venturing into the unknown. One of the nominated aircraft had a fuel gauging problem. "The left underwing tank is full but it indicates zero," I was reliably informed. The Form 700 showed total contents as if it were empty, but soothing noises from behind the counter saw me out of the line hut. Home weather was iffy, French Air Traffic Controllers were about to rescind the invitation for us to join their airspace, my number two had just been ordered out of the spare aircraft (they really must need these two aircraft back pronto) and, after all, I **had** given that tank a belt on the walkround and it sounded full. (Quack, quack).

What my heart knew and my nasty suspicious mind suspected was soon confirmed when I released the brakes on take-off and the aircraft veered grasswards, two tonnes out of balance. But yet, 50 kts, I soon corrected it; 80 kts, so perhaps; 100 kts, I had lined up a bit askew; 110 kts, and we do need the jet back home; 120 kts, and there is some cross wind; 130 kts, and if I abort now; 140 kts, what effect will this load have; 150 kts, when the thrust reverse goes out; 160 kts, and as for the cable; 170 kts, and in any case; 180 kts, we're airborne. (Quack, quack, quack).

Call me weird, but I feel safer in the air than I do on the ground, particularly on a runway with an unbalanced aircraft. Yet that final duckling was lining up to take its final nibble and, as the flaps travelled up, the CSAS roll channel dumped. Full left stick, a polished boot-full of rudder, silent running in the front, and still the right wing dropped. Just time for a glance down at the CSAS panel and a firm press on the failed lights and bingo - the mother of all pilot-induced oscillations as the fly-by-wire told the full fuel tank exactly who was boss.

The MASS finally went safe once we cleared the thunderstorm we could not avoid - because we had no radar because there were no spares because there was no air transport, but that's another chapter.

So to the lessons. **Don't Assume, Check**. I had assumed. There's no doubt I had plenty of doubts, but I chose to accept or, more accurately, to ignore them. **Abort in good time**; a good time to have aborted this sortie would have been at breakfast. So there's the rub - have you learnt anything from my close shave? Or would you, given a similar set of circumstances, find yourself in the same pickle?

GHOSTLY WIRES

LC

Having recently returned to Germany after a long absence from Army flying in BAOR, my attention was caught one evening by a floodlit Skeeter helicopter parked proudly on a plinth in Detmold. Closer inspection of the comical little warrior revealed its identity to be XL739 - and prompted me to consult the more disreputable end of my Log Book to see what XL739 was doing on a certain evening in 1966.

On that May evening, we had just come to the end of a two-week exercise on Soltau Training Area which had culminated in a long battle astride the pylon line that runs between Soltau and Luneburg. In support of one of the tank squadrons, I had spent a frustrating day trying to cover the frontage of the exercise, which involved climbing laboriously over the pylons to the inevitable cry of "Gotcha!" from the enemy. Flying under wires was strictly taboo in those days (*and today*), with the result that I finished the exercise with rather bruised morale.

It was a still, warm summer evening and since we weren't due to fly home until the following day the Flight Commander and I elected to take an aircraft each and do a little gentle continuation training. With doors off, one up and a full tank, XL739 was flying very sweetly and I found myself exploring the northern end of the Training Area with about an hour to spare and not much idea of how to spend it.

Just as I was about to turn for home, I spotted the same pylon line that had caused me so much frustration earlier in the day. I was alone, visibility was good and the setting sun was behind me. A glance at the wires from above prompted an irrational and totally unjustified desire to fly under them ... just this once.

There was no approved technique that I was aware of, and in my excitement at the challenge I decided that the most important thing was to get it done as quickly as possible. I chose the highest pylon I could find (it was enormous) and, aiming to pass beneath the wires about 20 yards away from the pylon itself, I set up a powered dive from about 500 ft.

I remember glancing briefly at the ASI as I pulled out of the dive and saw that I was just passing 100 kts as the pylon flashed by. Easing back on the stick at 105 kts, I looked up to see the sky almost blotted out with thick strands of cable.

They were so close together and so substantial that I could see, for a brief moment, the outline of individual strands of wire as my little Skeeter plunged through them. A reflex action grounded the collective lever with a jolt as I waited for the aircraft to fall apart around me.

Nothing happened. Frozen on to the controls in a muscular spasm, I allowed the Skeeter to climb gently as I murmured a variety of distress calls to myself and set up a forced landing pattern. Exploratory control movements revealed nothing untoward and as I carried out a powered landing I cursed myself for not checking that the area down-sun of the pylons was free of wires. After finding no material damage to the aircraft, I flew back to the scene of the crime at a safe height and combed the area for the wires I had flown through. Inexplicably, there were none.

Unable to unravel the mystery, I flew home and kept my mouth shut. A young inexperienced pilot who takes blatantly unnecessary risks is bad enough, but one who sees wires that don't exist clearly needs his head (and eyes) examined.

A couple of days passed before I mentioned the incident to anybody - and even then I was too appalled at my foolish behaviour to confide in my Flight Commander. The Flight Artificer listened to my story with a sardonic smile and produced the only explanation that could satisfactorily account for the strange occurrence.

The sun had been very low, very bright and directly astern. As I passed under the wires and raised the nose of the aircraft, the wires would have come between me and the sun. At that moment, their image would have been projected on to the canopy directly in front of me, no doubt greatly magnified by the curved line of the perspex.

I shall never forget the experience of that split-second. I'm just grateful that my first (and so far my last) wire strike turned out to be a phoney. The image of those wires has stayed with me ever since and my awareness of the wire hazard has remained undiminished despite the passage of time.

I was lucky. I learnt about low flying - and wires - from that.

Saro Skeeter AOP12

STOP STOP STOP...!

English Electric Lightning

This is a sorry tale of youthful enthusiasm combined with a good helping of folk lore. It stems from those halcyon days when the nearest thing to a computer was that produced by Dalton and issued to navigators! I'm talking about the time when the Lightning was based at Binbrook to protect Binbrook which was where the Lightnings were based.

Despite the rumours about the Lightning's limitation on range, we did occasionally make it as far as mainland Europe; usually to Gutersloh, which had been taken over by the Harrier fraternity and which had such an excellent cellar bar.

But before I take you off to the delights of Warsteiner, some points concerning Lightning folk lore. The Lightning was, surprisingly, a docile and forgiving beast in pure handling terms and was not burdened by such annoyances as AOA gauges (which would only have led to more irritating limitations and put an end to the 'Rotation' take-off) or navigators, although I have since revised my opinion of those paid up members of the Society of Directional Consultants. In fact, the Lightning was so docile that my pre-solo check consisted of a tight circuit competition with my QFI, culminating in his graciously allowing me to go solo as I had managed to get round finals in full reheat and with, what felt like, full pro-spin control. It is true to say that if your face fitted, it helped to ensure your successful graduation from the course. Of course, the bar was probably the best place to try and make your face fit and was also where you learnt all those unwritten tricks of the trade - the folk lore.

One of the more comical annual requirements for the Lightning was the spinning currency in the Jet Provost (the Lightning was not cleared for intentional spinning). Having sat in front of a cine projector, not a video, and watched "10 Seconds Is A Long Time", then climbed into a JP5 on a running turnround and launched into the ether, you were expected to put the JP into a spin and then recover. Oh yes, you were supposed to shout out to the QFI the Lightning recovery drill while actually carrying out the JP recovery drill. At the end of the day, when most of the Sqn pilots had done their 'spin', we would adjourn to the bar and regale each other with war stories. It was in the bar where I heard that 10,000 ft was far too high to be baling out of a spin (6,000 ft was the popular choice) and we heard rumours of one of the QFIs who, on every dual check, would deliberately spin the Lightning to prove its predictable handling.

Now it's time for the Warsteiner. I was Fully Operational, with 2 years on type and heading for Gutersloh as one of a pair, the other pilot being the Flt Cdr. We were deploying for a few days of dissimilar air combat training (DACT) with the Harriers. One the sortie in question we briefed with the Harrier pilot for a 2 v 1 DACT. Two Lightnings against one Harrier, I was thinking of turkey shoots. But the Harrier did have a trick or 2 available to him, notably the last ditch manoeuvre. This involved the Harrier putting the nozzles into the full braking stop position and, effectively, stopping in mid air. It was supposed to force the opponent to fly out in front, but did involve a high risk of collision. Because of the collision risk, the Harrier pilot repeatedly briefed the effect of the braking stop and that he may have to call "breakaway", which meant that he was in the braking stop, not sure where his aircraft was going to finish up and that the opponent should 'breakaway'. It sounded sensible to me!

At 12,000 ft, in the middle of a flight, we'd got the Harrier where we wanted him. Unfortunately, closing for that guns shot I didn't notice that he was in the braking stop until almost too late. In order to avoid the collision, I snatched the stick hard back and applied a bootfull of rudder with as much aileron deflection as I could get. It sounds like full pro-spin control - and that is exactly what happened; with the Harrier at the 'epicentre' of my spin. I even beat him to the call of "breakaway" as I thought he must have more control than me. Not to worry though, the spin recovery is easy and it's a beautiful day with a clear horizon. But, looking at the horizon, I was completely disorientated and could not tell which way the spin was going - the Lightning was never fitted with a turn needle and the spin was much more oscillatory than I had expected. Never mind, just centralise and wait. Remembering the message from the spinning film: spin recovery should take 10 seconds or 4 turns and 15 seconds or 6 turns if no rudder is applied"; I sat there waiting for the 6 turns to finish. I remember noting 10,000 ft on the altimeter after 2 of the turns, but folk lore said that 6,000 ft was ok to jump from. I then remember putting my hands on the ejector seat handle as I saw 8,000 ft on the altimeter. At 6,000 ft, I remember a lot of shouting on the radio, thinking to myself 'I'm going to be in trouble for ejecting', and starting to pull the handle. At that point the spin stopped! I pushed back down on the seat handle and pulled back on the stick instead. I must admit to being impressed by the ground rush in the last stages of the recovery and my Flt Cdr, very wisely, decided to call it a day and take us back to Gutersloh.

On the way back to Gutersloh, the Flt Cdr spotted my brake parachute cable had fallen out during the spin and had been burnt through by the jet efflux. He landed first, cleared the runway and I came in for a chuteless landing. The aircraft came to a stop with only a few feet of runway remaining and, once again, I was impressed with the rush of the barrier as I approached it, but stopped just short. We discussed the events of that trip and decided that I should sit out the next combat that day. Instead, while the Flt Cdr was airborne, I wangled a trip in a Harrier T4 on an air test and got to play with the braking stop. You may not be surprised to find out that I managed to get the Harrier to depart, but my Bona Mate in the front recovered it immediately.

Flight safety lessons? I learnt a few:

- ✈ Bar room folk lore is usually very interesting but that's all it is; a good war story.

- ✈ Limits are frequently set, and amended, as a result of somebody else's accident or incident. I nearly added to the case for raising the ejection height during a spin. Eject in time ... I nearly didn't make it back to write this article.

- ✈ Finally, be aware, particularly at that dangerous time of 500 hours on type, that you may have an over-inflated impression of your own capabilities.

For the record, should I ever spin again, I am leaving at 10,000 ft; no matter what they say in the bar!

English Electric Lightning

GLOSSARY

ACRONYM	MEANING
2ATAF	2nd Allied Tactical Air Force
700/F700/Form 700	Aircraft Engineering Record Book
A1	QFI 'Exceptional' grading
A2	QFI 'Above Average' grading
ACMI	Air Combat Manoeuvring Instrumentation
AEF	Air Experience Flight
AEW	Airborne Early Warning
AGL or agl	Above Ground Level
AI	Attitude Indicator
AIFG	Advanced Instrument Flying Grading
AMFO	Air Ministry Flying Order
AMSL	Above Mean Sea Level
AOA	Angle of Attack
AOC	Air Officer Commanding - a big boss
AOP	Air Observation Post
AP3225	QFI's Instructional Handbook
ASE	Auto Stabilisation Equipment
ASI	Air Speed Indicator
ASI	Air Staff Instruction
ASP	Aircraft Servicing Pan
ATC	Air Traffic Control
ATC	Air Training Corps
B1	QFI 'Average' grading
B2	QFI 'Probationary' grading
BAOR	British Army of the Rhine
BFT	Basic Flying Test
BFT	Basic Flying Training
BFTS	Basic Flying Training School
BHT	Basic Handling Test
CFI	Chief Flying Instructor
CFS	Central Flying School
cfs	Cadet Fight Sergeant
CONDOR	Confidential Direct Occurrence Report (sent directly to the Inspector of Flight Safety (RAF) for his eyes only)
Creamed off (QFI)	An exceptional student selected for a short instructional tour before his first operational tour
CSAS	Command Stability Augmentation System
CSRO	Combat Survival and Rescue Officer
DCFI	Deputy Chief Flying Instructor
DCO	Duty Carried Out - a successful mission
EFATO	Engine Failure After Take Off
F5060	Sortie Debrief Form
FL	Flight Level
FOB	Flying Order Book
FOB	Forward Operating Base
FOX1	Radar Missile Kill
FR	Fighter Reconnaissance
FRCs	Flight Reference Cards
FTS	Flying Training School
GCA	Ground Controlled Approach
GCI	Ground Controlled Intercept (also used for the Controller)
GEF	General Engineering Flight / Ground Electrical Flight

George	Autopilot
Goon Suit	Immersion Suit (waterproof overalls)
Gp1	Fast-jet Training
Gp2	Multi-engined Training
Gp3	Helicopter Training
GRF	Ground Radio Flight
HAS	Hardened Aircraft Shelter
HASELLs	Pre-Aerobatic Checks (Height, Airframe, Security, Engine, Location, Lookout)
HP Cock	High Pressure Fuel Cock
HUD	Head-Up Display
HYD 1 (or 2)	Hydraulic System 1 (or 2)
INAS	Inertial Navigation System
IME	Instrument Meteorological Conditions
IRE	Instrument Rating Examiner
ISS	Individual Studies School (Correspondence Staff Course)
JP	Jet Provost
JP	Junior Pilot (early 'first tourist')
Knock it off	'Cease Combat' Call
LP Cock	Low Pressure Fuel Cock
MA	Mission Accomplished (DCO)
MASS	Master Armament Safety Switch
Meatbox	Meteor Aircraft
MFR	Military Flying Regulation
Mineval	Station Evaluation Exercise (Run internally)
Maxeval	Station Evaluation Exercise (Run by external agency)
MODFO	Ministry of Defence Flying Order
MTA	Military Training Area
OC OPS Wg / Sqn	Officer Commanding Operations Wing / Squadron - the Airfield Manager
OCU	Operational Conversion Unit
ORP	Operational Readiness Pan/Platform
PAN	Emergency call - lower priority than MAYDAY
Pandora	RAF Flight Safety Incident and Accident Database
PDQ	Pretty Damn Quick
PPL	Private Pilot's Licence
PR	Photographic Reconnaissance
QFI	Qualified Flying Instructor
QHI	Qualified Helicopter Instructor
QRA or 'Q'	Quick Reaction Alert
QWI	Qualified Weapon Instructor
RB199	Rolls Royce / Tornado Engine
RLG	Relief Landing Ground
SAC	Strategic Air Command
SAR	Search And Rescue
SFSO	Station Flight Safety Officer
SOC	Sector Operations Centre
SOP	Standard Operating Procedure
SSC	Short Service Commission (usually 8 or 12 years)
State 2	Precautionary airfield emergency readiness state
TACAN	Navigation equipment giving range and bearing from a selected beacon
TWU	Tactical Weapons Unit
UAS	University Air Squadron
UP	Unusual Position
VFR	Visual Flight Rules
VIB caption	A caption warning of possible engine vibration
VNE	Velocity Never (to) Exceed

A final thanks to all the authors who contributed the articles used in this book.
They obviously learnt about flying from their experiences - I hope you did too.

Wing Commander S H P Spry